Windows 8 App Projects

XAML and C# Edition

Nico Vermeir

Apress

Windows 8 App Projects: XAML and C# Edition

ISBN-13 (pbk): 978-1-4302-5065-4

ISBN-13 (electronic): 978-1-4302-5066-1

President and Publisher: Paul Manning
Lead Editor: Jonathan Hassell
Developmental Editor: Kate Blackham
Technical Reviewer: Kevin Dockx
Editorial Board: Steve Anglin, Mark Beckner, Ewan Buckingham, Gary Cornell, Louise Corrigan,
    Morgan Ertel, Jonathan Gennick, Jonathan Hassell, Robert Hutchinson, Michelle Lowman,
    James Markham, Matthew Moodie, Jeff Olson, Jeffrey Pepper, Douglas Pundick, Ben Renow-Clarke,
    Dominic Shakeshaft, Gwenan Spearing, Matt Wade, Tom Welsh
Coordinating Editor: Katie Sullivan
Copy Editor: Mary Bearden
Compositor: SPi Global
Indexer: SPi Global
Artist: SPi Global
Cover Designer: Anna Ishchenko

Distributed to the book trade worldwide by Springer Science+Business Media New York, 233 Spring Street, 6th Floor, New York, NY 10013. Phone 1-800-SPRINGER, fax (201) 348-4505, e-mail orders-ny@springer-sbm.com, or visit www.springeronline.com. Apress Media, LLC is a California LLC and the sole member (owner) is Springer Science + Business Media Finance Inc (SSBM Finance Inc). SSBM Finance Inc is a Delaware corporation.

For information on translations, please e-mail rights@apress.com, or visit www.apress.com.

Apress and friends of ED books may be purchased in bulk for academic, corporate, or promotional use. eBook versions and licenses are also available for most titles. For more information, reference our Special Bulk Sales-eBook Licensing web page at www.apress.com/bulk-sales.

Any source code or other supplementary materials referenced by the author in this text is available to readers at www.apress.com. For detailed information about how to locate your book's source code, go to www.apress.com/source-code/.

Contents at a Glance

Contents

About the Author

Nico Vermeir is an MCP living in Belgium. He is currently employed as a NET mobile developer in the Mobile Solution Center at RealDolmen, one of Belgium's leading IT single source providers, where he focuses on developing apps for Windows Phone and Windows 8. He is also a founding member and board member of the Belgian Metro App Developer Network, a user group focused on Windows 8 and Windows Phone development. Since June 2012 he has been a proud member of Microsoft's Extended Experts Team Belgium. If you're in Belgium, feel free to drop by an event: http://www.madn.be.

About the Technical Reviewer

Kevin Dockx lives in Belgium and works at RealDolmen, one of Belgium's biggest ICT companies. He is a 31-year-old technical specialist/project leader on NET (web) applications, mainly XAML based, and a solution owner for Windows 8 Store applications. His main focus lies in all things XAML, but he still keeps an eye on the new developments concerning other products from the Microsoft NET (Web) Stack. As an XAML enthusiast, he's a regular speaker at various national and international events, such as Microsoft Techdays in Belgium, Portugal, and Finland and VISUG and MADN events, Simplicity Day, Community Day, among others.

He also writes articles for various XAML-related sites, and he wrote a best-selling Silverlight book, Packt Publishing's *Silverlight 4 Data and Services Cookbook* (`https://www.packtpub.com/microsoft-silverlight-4-data-and-services-cookbook/book`) and its follow-up, the *Silverlight 5 Data and Services Cookbook* (`www.packtpub.com/microsoft-silverlight-5-data-and-services-cookbook/book`). His blog, which contains various tidbits on XAML, NET, and occasional ramblings, can be found at `http://blog.kevindockx.com/`, and you can contact him on Twitter via @KevinDockx.

Acknowledgments

I would like to thank my wife, Kim, for letting me chase my dreams, no matter how crazy or how many lonely evenings it meant for her.

I would also like to thank Kevin Dockx for being my technical reviewer and always being there to help or give advice. I already learned a great deal from him and I sincerely hope we'll be working together for many years to come.

And last but not least I would like to thank the Belgian Microsoft developers evangelist team for helping me with test devices, advice, awesome events, and for supporting our great Belgian communities.

CHAPTER 1

■ ■ ■

Introduction

Windows 8 is an exciting release. It tries to reimagine the way we use computers; it's a fresh wind through an old, established environment. Before we dive into the technical stuff, we'll have a small history lesson about the development process of Windows 8.

History

Windows 8 was first announced at the Consumer Electronics Show (CES) in 2011. Back then, it was just the next Windows iteration. A very early version found its way onto the Internet pretty fast, and inside was evidence of native Universal Serial Bus (USB) 3.0 support, United Extensible Firmware Interface (UEFI), and even some slight hints at an application (app) store. The leaked version still had the classic Start button and Start menu like in Windows 7. The biggest news, however, was not really the announcement of the new operating system but the fact that Windows was getting an Acom RISC Machine (ARM) version next to the classic x86/x64 versions. This immediately fueled rumors of Windows 8 focusing on touch and taking on capabilities of the iPad and Android tablets.

A few months later Microsoft showed off the new interface for the first time at the Taipei Computex 2011 show. This was followed closely by the Build Windows 8 blog, where the Windows 8 product team would reflect on certain decisions and features involving Windows 8.

On September 13, 2011, the keynote presentation of the Build conference went into detail about the Windows 8 app store and the development process. Microsoft Belgium asked all their technical communities to set up a live stream for their members. I remember sitting there and getting really excited about getting started developing for this brand new platform with a potential huge reach of customers.

In that same keynote there was an announcement of the Windows 8 Developer Preview, marking the start of one of the biggest beta programs of any Windows release so far. The Developer Preview came with Visual Studio 2012 beta (known as Visual Studio 11 back then) and a Blend 5 beta, giving developers the chance to dive into the platform early on before release. It also included some installed example apps that had been developed by interns at Microsoft. The Developer Preview did not yet have an app store, but its sole purpose was to get developers familiar with the new Windows Software Development Kit. The operating system and Visual Studio bits were still in a very early stage, resulting in many crashes and frustration among those trying to learn the new development environment.

The Developer Preview, shown in Figure 1-1, still had a Start button, it was square this time but it was still there. It would take the user to the Start screen, so the classic menu was already gone. A registry hack appeared on the Web faster then you could say metro. That hack brought back the classic Windows 7 shell.

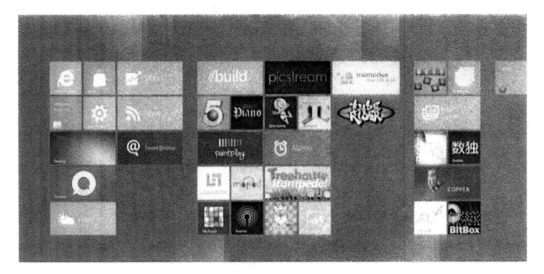

Figure 1-1. *Developer Preview*

In February 2012 Microsoft announced the Windows 8 Consumer Preview, as shown in Figure 1-2. This version was aimed toward normal users to get them familiar with the new interface. In this version the Start button was gone, but other than that it still strongly resembled Windows 7 with all the glass effects. Developers were able to get a new Visual Studio 11 beta version and could actually get work done on this. There was an increase in stability in both Windows and Visual Studio. Microsoft reported that the Consumer Preview was downloaded over 1 million times in 24 hours, making it one of the most popular beta products ever released by the software company.

Figure 1-2. *Consumer Preview*

June 2012 marked the release of the last beta version, called the Windows 8 Release Preview. The Release Preview, as shown in Figure 1-3, included a multitude of apps and a working app store. Developers had to go through a long process with both their local Microsoft evangelists and the Microsoft test team before they could get their apps in the store.

Figure 1-3. *Release Preview*

The final version of Windows 8 was released to Microsoft Developer Network (MSDN) and Technet subscribers in August 2012 with general availability in October.

After this quick history lesson, we'll have a look at the internals of Windows 8 and the available application programming interfaces (APIs). The information in this chapter is accurate at the time of writing but, as with any software, might change over time. The best place to check if this information is still up to date is the MSDN documentation.

Windows Application Programming Interface

At Build, the chart presented in Figure 1-4 was shown to the public, laying out the differences between desktop applications and Windows Store apps.

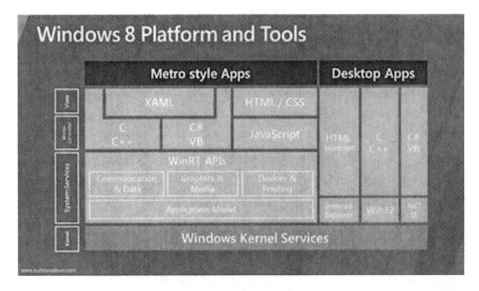

Figure 1-4. *Windows 8 Platform overview*

This image came with the announcement of different technologies for building Windows Store apps. We can use C, C++, C#, and Visual Basic to develop apps with Extensible Application Markup Language as the design language or use JavaScript with HyperText Markup Language (HTML) and Cascading Style Sheets (CSS). The fact that JavaScript and HTML can be used to develop apps meant that, in theory, web developers could hop on the bandwagon and start developing Windows Store apps. In reality they do have to learn some platform-specific stuff, but it should be quite easy to get started.

The image also shows that the Windows Store apps (still called Metro back then) and Desktop apps are both built on top of the Windows kernel, but they live in separate environments and have their own specific API set. A good example to prove this is the use of the webcam. Ever tried accessing a webcam from .NET? It requires interop calls to the avicap32 DLL, there are a bunch of wrappers, but it's still quite a pain to get it working. In a Windows Store app, you need two lines of code to show a webcam stream, as shown in Listing 1-1.

Listing 1-1. Accessing a Webcam in a Windows Store App

```
var dialog = new CameraCaptureUI();
await dialog.CaptureFileAsync(CameraCaptureUIMode.PhotoOrVideo);
```

Quite the difference! In the meantime, there has been some success in using the Windows Store API set in normal .NET applications using reflection, but to get those applications to work you need all users to have Windows 8.

About This Book

This book is for people who already know their way around in C#. It's aimed at developers who want to build and publish apps for Windows 8. Throughout this book, we'll only use C# for the code and XAML for the user interface. I try to explain everything by giving real-life examples and situations where a certain feature might come in handy.

Throughout the book we'll look at topics such as charms, data (both remote and local data), live tiles, notifications, and even some about game development.

Should you have any questions, comments, or remarks, feel free to share them with me on Twitter (http://www.twitter.com/NicoVermeir) or on my blog (http://www.spikie.be).

I'm ready if you are, let's get our journey started!

CHAPTER 2

▓ ▓ ▓

Getting Started

I hope you're just as excited as I am to dive into a wild Windows 8 adventure. Before we do, however, we need to get our development environment ready. When talking about developing in a Microsoft ecosystem, we of course are talking about Visual Studio. When developing Windows Store apps, the all new Visual Studio 2012 is the way to go, really the only way to go! Visual Studio 2010 has no support for the Windows 8 Software Development Kit (SDK) nor does Windows 7. So we need a machine running Windows 8, not Windows RT, and Visual Studio 2012.

Visual Studio 2012 comes in many flavors, some free, some rather expensive, but all very useful. The most complete Visual Studio version is of course the most expensive one, Visual Studio 2012 Ultimate. With Visual Studio 2012 Ultimate, you get all the features, including IntelliTrace debugging, load testing tools, Architecture Explorer, and many more features.

Visual Studio 2012 Premium has a lot of features but is missing the features mentioned above. It is still a very complete and good development environment that has everything needed to develop projects ranging from large, business-size applications to small mobile applications.

Visual Studio 2012 Professional is missing a lot of testing features and tools that the more expensive versions have, but it still has unit testing. Also lab management is not available nor are sprint planning in Team Foundation Server (TFS) and support for TFS as a service. It is still powerful enough for hobby developers and those working on smaller projects, but it might be best to upgrade to a more expensive version for really big projects.

If you do not have access to a Visual Studio license or do not want to invest in a license, there is always the Visual Studio Express edition, which is a collection of free Visual Studio versions each targeting a specific technology. There is a Visual Studio Express for web development, Windows Phone development, Windows Desktop development, and Windows 8 development. Since the introduction of Visual Studio 2012, there's also a Team Foundation Server Express edition if you want to work in a team or are in need of a self-administered source control system.

So choose your weapon (or environment) of choice and let's get those bits installed! Throughout this book I'll be using Visual Studio 2012 Premium, so screenshots might differ from your environment, especially if you're using Visual Studio Express, but other than some options being in a different spot, there shouldn't be much difference between what is shown in this book using Visual Studio 2012 Premium and the results for Visual Studio 2012 Express.

Setting Up the Environment

As of the 2012 version of Visual Studio, there are two types of installers. There's the complete installation on DVD, or ISO file, and there is a web installer that will download the necessary setup files on the fly. If you have a fast and stable broadband connection, the web installer definitely is the way to go as the download speed will be higher than the reading speed of a DVD drive. Grab your preferred installer and launch it, and the new Visual Studio logo and splash screen should welcome you, as shown in Figure 2-1.

Figure 2-1. *Visual Studio logo and splash screen*

I must say the new installer looks really great and has some smooth animations. This was actually the first time that I felt the long installation time of Visual Studio was worth the wait (Figure 2-2).

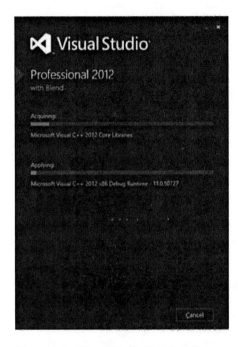

Figure 2-2. *Visual Studio 2012 installer*

If you keep looking at the installer, you should see a Windows 8 reference passing by. The installer will detect whether or not you're installing Visual Studio 2012 on a Windows 8 machine. If you are, then the Windows 8 SDK will be installed automatically with Visual Studio.

The Windows 8 SDK is available as a separate download at http://msdn.microsoft.com/en-us/windows/hardware/hh852363.aspx. A major difference with previous Windows SDKs is that the Windows 8 SDK no longer has a built-in command line compiler. That means if you want to use another integrated development environment (IDE) other than Visual Studio (technically, you can even develop apps in Notepad as long as you have a compiler to run your code through) to develop Windows 8 apps, you will have to make sure that it contains a compiler or that you have one installed on your system.

Included in the SDK are tools, libraries, and headers required to build Windows 8 apps using C#, Visual Basic .NET (VB.NET), and C++ using Extensible Application Markup Language (XAML) for markup or JavaScript and HTML5 as markup. One of the most useful tools in the SDK is the Windows App Certification Kit (WACK). This is a program that runs a set of tests on your app. Running the WACK is actually one of the first things the Windows 8 app test team does when you submit an application to the store. We'll delve deeper into the WACK in Chapter 11 of this book, for now just remember that it's important to run this before you submit your app to the store to save you loads of time.

Once your Visual Studio setup is complete, start it up and click New Project. If all went well, you should see Windows Store under your favorite language in the Installed Templates tree, as shown in Figure 2-3.

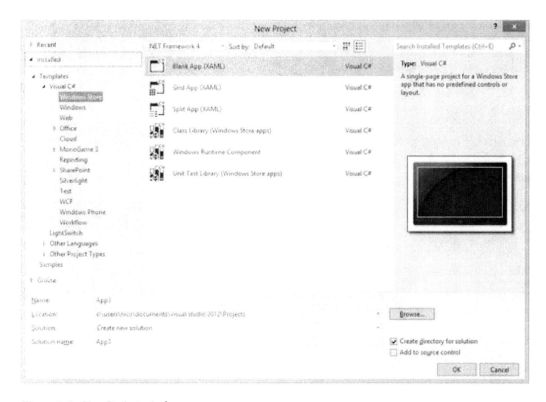

Figure 2-3. *New Project window*

If you're not seeing the Windows Store option, make sure you're looking under a supported Windows Store language (C#, VB.NET, C++, and JavaScript, there is no F# support at the time of writing). Also make sure you are running Windows 8 and that you didn't uncheck Windows Store apps during Visual Studio setup.

We're now basically good to go. You can install your favorite Visual Studio plug-ins if they have a Visual Studio 2012 version. I can't hardly live without Jetbrain's ReSharper, which extends Visual Studio in such a way that refactoring big chunks of code is a breeze, and navigating big projects becomes really easy. I personally feel that the key scheme of ReSharper feels better than that of Visual Studio. ReSharper also includes StyleCop, which is a plug-in that checks if your code is formatted the way it should be (pascal case or camel case where needed). There are other tools that have the same functionality if you decide to use them, so find the one that you feel most comfortable with. There is no best or worst plug-in. Also, don't go searching for the Visual Studio Productivity Power Tools that made Visual Studio 2010 so awesome. They don't exist for Visual Studio 2012 because they are integrated into the default setup, including the Solution Explorer, with a serious performance boost.

Now that we're all set up, let's take a look at the different templates that are included in the Windows 8 SDK. As the title mentions, this book only focuses on C# and XAML. The XAML in the book can also be used for Visual Basic and C++ projects, but the code will need to be converted to the language of your choice. I hope you're as excited as I am to get started, and I sincerely hope that I can carry some of my passion and love for this platform to you. Enough text, let's get coding!

Starting a First Project

The Windows 8 SDK comes with different templates that start you off with certain layout, navigation, and test data. Should your app design follow more or less the same layout as one of the templates, it provides you with an easy set up and allows you to skip over writing some boilerplate code for the navigation logic. However, don't just adjust the template and submit the app. Alter the app's design to make it your own. Your app on the Windows Store is your signature. No one looks at the developer name on the Windows Store, but rather they look at the quality of other apps built by the same person. Your apps build your reputation, not your name. Figure 2-4 gives an overview of the available templates in the Windows 8 SDK.

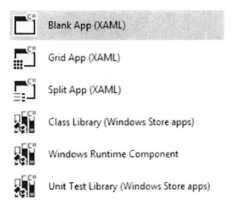

Figure 2-4. *Default templates included in the SDK*

We'll start with the last three templates and then go back to the first three.

■ **Note**   The code in the templates is great for reference, but they generally don't use best practices. I would greatly advise you to start from a blank template and add a basic page to the project. Visual Studio will add some classes and resource dictionaries to the project. From there you will have a great starting point for your trademark application.

Class Library

The first one, Class Library, should be pretty familiar to those who've already worked with .NET. It's basically a project filled with classes and functions that you can use inside your Windows Store app or even share between different apps. When a Class Library gets built, it results in an assembly. That assembly can be used in applications that target the same framework version. The big advantage here is that we can create a class with common functions, which is often needed in apps. We create the Class Library once and reference it in the apps that need its logic. Class Libraries exist for any type of .NET application, just make sure both the library and the app target the same framework version.

Windows Runtime Component

A Windows Runtime Component is basically the same as a Class Library. The big difference is that a Windows Runtime Component can be shared between any language that is supported by Windows Store development, as long as it's in a Windows Store app. That means that some very intensive tasks can be developed in C++ as a

Windows Runtime Component, and that component can then be called on in, for example, a JavaScript or a C# app. Also background tasks rely on runtime components as they can only be built as a runtime component. This will be discussed more later in the book. The example presented here is actually used in some apps because C++ is a native code and it has more performance than managed code such as C#. If you want to read more about the Windows Runtime Component, including best practices and possible traps, look at the MSDN documentation at `http://msdn.microsoft.com/en-us/library/windows/apps/br230301(v=vs.110).aspx`.

Unit Test Library

A Unit Test Library is just that, a library that should be filled with tests that will test your business logic. If you build your tests just right, you wouldn't need to run the app every time you change your logic, so you could just run the test and see if the result is what you had expected. Let's say, for example, you have a class that generates a discount based on what customers have already purchased in the past. At a certain moment in time, that logic will change, and if there are tests available in the project, you would only need to adjust the logic and the expected result in the test and run it. A test that takes a second to complete is better than having to run the app, log in, select a customer, and so on.

With that you should now have some background information about these three project types. I won't be going into detail about these because we won't actually use them in the book. Now let's take a look at the project templates.

Blank App Template

First up is the Blank App Template. This is literally a blank app, with barely any code inside the template. When you run it, all you'll get is a black screen. The file `MainPage.xaml` is the first page of your app that will appear. If you want, you can change the startup page in `App.xaml.cs`. The `OnLaunched` event creates the page instance. In the Blank App Template, it looks like the code in Listing 2-1.

Listing 2-1. MainPage.xaml

```
<Page
    x:Class="App3.MainPage"
    xmlns="http://schemas.microsoft.com/winfx/2006/xaml/presentation"
    xmlns:x="http://schemas.microsoft.com/winfx/2006/xaml"
    xmlns:local="using:App3"
    xmlns:d="http://schemas.microsoft.com/expression/blend/2008"
    xmlns:mc="http://schemas.openxmlformats.org/markup-compatibility/2006"
    mc:Ignorable="d">

    <Grid Background="{StaticResource ApplicationPageBackgroundThemeBrush}">

    </Grid>
</Page>
```

As you can see, the only thing there is a grid. All your page controls need to go in that grid, however, you are free to change it from a grid to a stack panel or any other container. Listing 2-2 shows the code behind the file `MainPage.xaml`, called `MainPage.xaml.cs`.

Listing 2-2. MainPage.xaml.cs

```
using Windows.UI.Xaml.Controls;
using Windows.UI.Xaml.Navigation;

// The Blank Page item template is documented at http://go.microsoft.com/fwlink/?LinkId=234238

namespace App3
{
    /// <summary>
    /// An empty page that can be used on its own or navigated to within a Frame.
    /// </summary>
    public sealed partial class MainPage : Page
    {
        public MainPage()
        {
            this.InitializeComponent();
        }

        /// <summary>
        /// Invoked when this page is about to be displayed in a Frame.
        /// </summary>
        /// <param name="e">Event data that describes how this page was reached. The Parameter
        /// property is typically used to configure the page.</param>
        protected override void OnNavigatedTo(NavigationEventArgs e)
        {
        }
    }
}
```

All there is here is a default constructor that initializes all the controls on the page and an event handler for when the app navigates to the page. As you can see, the MainPage inherits from the Page base class. Page is a user control that defines properties for both the bottom and top app bar, a frame where all the content will be shown, and the NavigationCacheMode. That latter allows us to cache every page in memory. When navigating back to a cached page, the app will load the cached page instead of instantiating a new instance. Next to those properties, the Page class also holds three virtual methods: OnNavigatedFrom, OnNavigatedTo, and OnNavigatingFrom. These are perfect for passing data between pages or saving settings or data when navigating away from a page.

Grid App Template

The Grid App Template consists of three pages. The app starts at the GroupedItemsPage (this is defined in App.xaml.cs, in the OnLaunched method), a page consisting of a GridView (Figure 2-5). The GridView allows for items to be grouped, for example, a list of cities can be grouped into countries. We'll take a deeper look at the GridView later in the book.

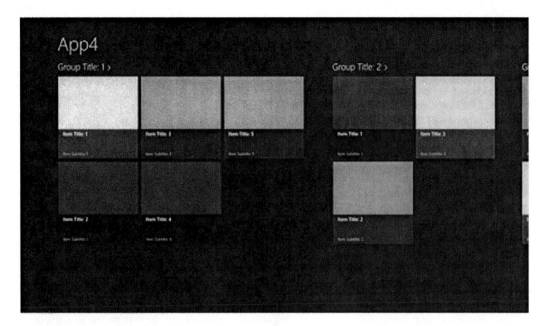

Figure 2-5. *Grid App Template main page*

This image clearly shows the groups. Notice that the groups have an angle bracket (>) next to their name. That's because the group titles provide the link to the group details. One of the design guidelines Microsoft proposes is to use as much content as possible for navigation, providing a much cleaner layout without excessive use of buttons or other navigational controls. The CollectionViewSource allows us to do stuff like grouping and sorting items in a collection without having to write the logic ourselves. The CollectionViewSource takes in our items, applies any sorting or grouping, and creates a view. We can then bind the CollectionViewSource to a control like a GridView to display that view, as shown in Listing 2-3.

Listing 2-3. CollectionViewSource in Grid App Template

```
<Page.Resources>
        <CollectionViewSource
            x:Name="groupedItemsViewSource"
            Source="{Binding Groups}"
            IsSourceGrouped="true"
            ItemsPath="TopItems"
            d:Source="{Binding AllGroups, Source={d:DesignInstance Type=data:SampleDataSource,
IsDesignTimeCreatable=True}}"/>
    </Page.Resources>
```

Notice the bindings there? The controls on this page get their information from the DefaultViewModel, which is set as the DataContext for this page. Feeling a bit lost there? Let me explain. An XAML page or element can have a DataContext, a class that contains a bunch of properties, commands, and other stuff that holds the data and logic for this page or element. When we define a binding on an element's property, we attach the value from the property on the DataContext to the property on that element. Take the CollectionViewSource in Listing 2-3 for example. The Source property is bound to a property called Groups. That property can be found on something called the DefaultViewModel, as you can see in Listing 2-4. When working with XAML applications, it's really important to have a good understanding of data binding, which we'll discuss more in depth when we're talking about Model View ViewModel.

Listing 2-4. DataContext Set on a Page

```
<common:LayoutAwarePage
    x:Name="pageRoot"
    x:Class="App4.GroupedItemsPage"
    DataContext="{Binding DefaultViewModel, RelativeSource={RelativeSource Self}}"
    xmlns="http://schemas.microsoft.com/winfx/2006/xaml/presentation"
    xmlns:x="http://schemas.microsoft.com/winfx/2006/xaml"
    xmlns:local="using:App4"
    xmlns:data="using:App4.Data"
    xmlns:common="using:App4.Common"
    xmlns:d="http://schemas.microsoft.com/expression/blend/2008"
    xmlns:mc="http://schemas.openxmlformats.org/markup-compatibility/2006"
    mc:Ignorable="d">
```

Also notice that a page in the Blank Template was of type Page, while in this template it's of type LayoutAwarePage.

LayoutAwarePage

The LayoutAwarePage class lives in the Common folder inside the solution. The class inherits from Page, the same class as was used in the Blank Template folder. The most important functions in this class are the GoBack and GoHome functions. The GoBack method is what takes care of the Back button found on the pages in this project template. GoHome navigates the user to the top page on the current navigation stack. The page title and Back button are also present in the template, and they are usually found closer to the bottom of the page (Listing 2-5). Next to that, the LayoutAwarePage class also handles orientation changes, full to snap mode changes, and saving and loading page state. We'll take a closer look at those functions when we discuss orientation changes later in the book.

Listing 2-5. LayoutAwarePage Back Button and Page Title

```
<!-- Back button and page title -->
      <Grid>
          <Grid.ColumnDefinitions>
              <ColumnDefinition Width="Auto"/>
              <ColumnDefinition Width="*"/>
          </Grid.ColumnDefinitions>
          <Button x:Name="backButton" Click="GoBack" IsEnabled="{Binding Frame.CanGoBack,
ElementName=pageRoot}" Style="{StaticResource BackButtonStyle}"/>
          <TextBlock x:Name="pageTitle" Text="{StaticResource AppName}" Grid.Column="1"
IsHitTestVisible="false" Style="{StaticResource PageHeaderTextStyle}"/>
      </Grid>
```

Notice that the IsEnabled property of the Back button is bound to the Frame.CanGoBack. Frame is the control that the pages are displayed in. It loads new pages and holds the navigation stack. If the CanGoBack property is false, that means the current page is the top page on the navigation stack, effectively hiding the button.

GroupDetailPage

When you click one of the group titles, the app will navigate to the GroupDetailPage, as shown in Figure 2-6.

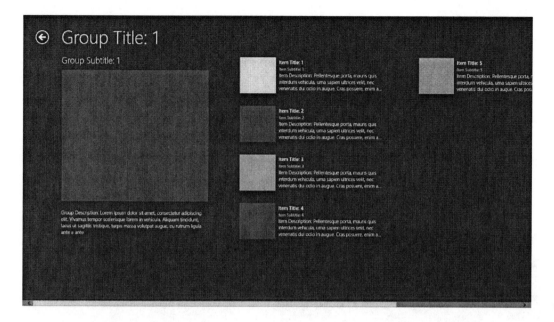

Figure 2-6. *GroupDetailPage*

This page consist of a GridView, just like the GroupedItemsPage, only this time the GridView has a header (the big image with description text under it on the left of the page). Listing 2-6 presents the code associated with the GroupDetailsPage.

Listing 2-6. GroupDetailsPage GridView

```
<GridView
            x:Name="itemGridView"
            AutomationProperties.AutomationId="ItemGridView"
            AutomationProperties.Name="Items In Group"
            TabIndex="1"
            Grid.RowSpan="2"
            Padding="120,126,120,50"
            ItemsSource="{Binding Source={StaticResource itemsViewSource}}"
            ItemTemplate="{StaticResource Standard500x130ItemTemplate}"
            SelectionMode="None"
            IsSwipeEnabled="false"
            IsItemClickEnabled="True"
            ItemClick="ItemView_ItemClick">

        <GridView.Header>
            <StackPanel Width="480" Margin="0,4,14,0">
                <TextBlock Text="{Binding Subtitle}" Margin="0,0,18,20"
Style="{StaticResource SubheaderTextStyle}" MaxHeight="60"/>
                <Image Source="{Binding Image}" Height="400" Margin="0,0,18,20"
Stretch="UniformToFill" AutomationProperties.Name="{Binding Title}"/>
                <TextBlock Text="{Binding Description}" Margin="0,0,18,0"
Style="{StaticResource BodyTextStyle}"/>
```

13

```
            </StackPanel>
        </GridView.Header>
        <GridView.ItemContainerStyle>
            <Style TargetType="FrameworkElement">
                <Setter Property="Margin" Value="52,0,0,10"/>
            </Style>
        </GridView.ItemContainerStyle>
    </GridView>
```

ItemDetailPage

When one of the items in the list is clicked, the app navigates to the third and final page in this template, the ItemDetailPage, as shown in Figure 2-7.

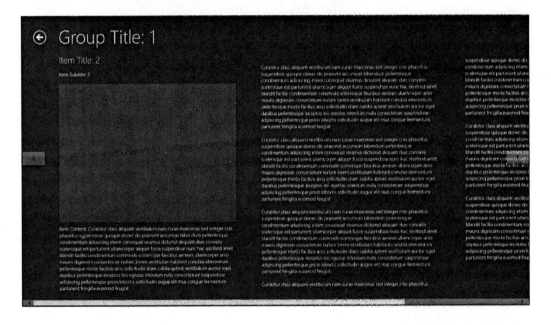

Figure 2-7. *ItemDetailPage*

See the arrows on both side of the page? They allow us to flip back and forth between all the items in the collection. That way we won't have to navigate to the previous page to select another item, and we can just flip until we get the one we need. This is done by using the FlipView control, as presented in Listing 2-7, which spans the entire page.

Listing 2-7. FlipView

```
<FlipView
        x:Name="flipView"
        AutomationProperties.AutomationId="ItemsFlipView"
        AutomationProperties.Name="Item Details"
        TabIndex="1"
```

```
        Grid.RowSpan="2"
        ItemsSource="{Binding Source={StaticResource itemsViewSource}}">

        <FlipView.ItemContainerStyle>
            <Style TargetType="FlipViewItem">
                <Setter Property="Margin" Value="0,137,0,0"/>
            </Style>
        </FlipView.ItemContainerStyle>

        <FlipView.ItemTemplate>
            <DataTemplate>
            ...
        </DataTemplate>
        </FlipView.ItemTemplate>
</FlipView>
```

That was a quick overview of the Grid App Template, so now let's take a look at the last template that is included in the Windows 8 SDK.

Split App Template

The Split App Template consists of two pages. The first one is the ItemsPage, which consists of nothing more than a GridView. It's quite similar to the GroupedItemsPage, the only difference being that the GridView on this page isn't grouped, and it's pretty easy to adjust the page so that it has groups if you want them. A simple example where this can be used is a feed reader, as shown in Figure 2-8. The first page shows the headlines, and clicking a headline navigates to the second page showing the complete text with a small list of all the other headlines, making it very easy for the user to read the next article.

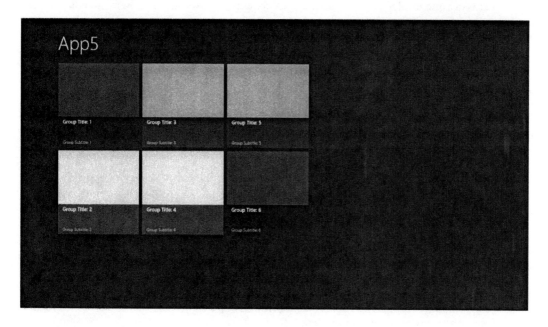

Figure 2-8. *Split App MainPage*

By the way, don't worry too much about the VisualState stuff on the pages in the templates. This will be discussed in detail in Chapter 8. The ItemsPage has nothing that is new to us, so let's just skip it and go straight to the SplitPage, as shown in Figure 2-9.

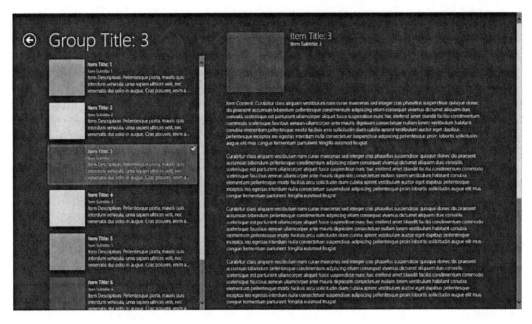

Figure 2-9. *SplitPage*

The SplitPage consists of a grid divided into two columns, one containing a list with all the items and the second containing the information from the items. This setup is perfect for an RSS reader or a sports app.

The list of items is contained in a ListView, as presented in Listing 2-8.

Listing 2-8. ListView

```
<!-- Vertical scrolling item list -->
    <ListView
        x:Name="itemListView"
        AutomationProperties.AutomationId="ItemsListView"
        AutomationProperties.Name="Items"
        TabIndex="1"
        Grid.Row="1"
        Margin="-10,-10,0,0"
        Padding="120,0,0,60"
        ItemsSource="{Binding Source={StaticResource itemsViewSource}}"
        IsSwipeEnabled="False"
        SelectionChanged="ItemListView_SelectionChanged"
        ItemTemplate="{StaticResource Standard130ItemTemplate}"/>
```

The ItemsSource set in this ListView is a CollectionViewSource, just like in the Grid Template. The text for each item appears in the second column of the grid and is placed in a ScrollViewer, a control that allows text or images that fall off the screen to be scrollable, as presented in Listing 2-9.

Listing 2-9. ScrollViewer

```xml
<!-- Details for selected item -->
        <ScrollViewer
            x:Name="itemDetail"
            AutomationProperties.AutomationId="ItemDetailScrollViewer"
            Grid.Column="1"
            Grid.RowSpan="2"
            Padding="70,0,120,0"
            DataContext="{Binding SelectedItem, ElementName=itemListView}"
            d:DataContext="{Binding AllGroups[0].Items[0], Source={d:DesignInstance
Type=data:SampleDataSource, IsDesignTimeCreatable=True}}"
            Style="{StaticResource VerticalScrollViewerStyle}">

            <Grid x:Name="itemDetailGrid" Margin="0,60,0,50">
                <Grid.RowDefinitions>
                    <RowDefinition Height="Auto"/>
                    <RowDefinition Height="Auto"/>
                    <RowDefinition Height="*"/>
                </Grid.RowDefinitions>
                <Grid.ColumnDefinitions>
                    <ColumnDefinition Width="Auto"/>
                    <ColumnDefinition Width="*"/>
                </Grid.ColumnDefinitions>

                <Image Grid.Row="1" Margin="0,0,20,0" Width="180" Height="180"
Source="{Binding Image}" Stretch="UniformToFill" AutomationProperties.Name="{Binding Title}"/>
                <StackPanel x:Name="itemDetailTitlePanel" Grid.Row="1" Grid.Column="1">
                    <TextBlock x:Name="itemTitle" Margin="0,-10,0,0" Text="{Binding Title}"
Style="{StaticResource SubheaderTextStyle}"/>
                    <TextBlock x:Name="itemSubtitle" Margin="0,0,0,20" Text="{Binding Subtitle}"
Style="{StaticResource SubtitleTextStyle}"/>
                </StackPanel>
                <TextBlock Grid.Row="2" Grid.ColumnSpan="2" Margin="0,20,0,0"
Text="{Binding Content}" Style="{StaticResource BodyTextStyle}"/>
            </Grid>
        </ScrollViewer>
```

The ScrollViewer on the SplitPage has a grid as a child containing an image, title, subtitle, and the content. As soon as the grid becomes taller than the page, the ScrollViewer will do its magic and provide a scrollbar for the user. Obviously, it also provides kinetic scrolling on touch-enabled devices.

With that we conclude our quick overview of the templates that are included in the Windows 8 SDK. Let's take a look at the simulator next.

A Closer Look at the Simulator

If you've ever done mobile development, you probably understand the principle of emulators, a software version of the device you're developing for. The biggest advantage of an emulator is that you don't need a physical device to be able to test your app. One of the biggest disadvantages of using emulators is that they run on hardware that is much more powerful than the actual devices, providing a false sense of performance. My advice for every developer is feel free to use the emulator to test your app during development, but be sure to test it on an actual device before submitting the app to the store. This advice isn't just for developers that target the Microsoft platforms. Testing on actual devices is equally important for iOS and Android developers (actually Android developer should test on a multitude of devices because not every app works the same way on every device).

You may have noticed that I'm not talking about an emulator for Windows 8 but rather about a simulator. The big difference there is that an emulator actually contains an image of the full iOS it's emulating; for Windows 8 that would mean running Windows 8 inside of Windows 8, and that can easily be done with a virtual machine. Microsoft decided otherwise, so in order to save resources, the simulator actually uses your Windows 8 installation. The simulator is actually a thin client that remote desktops into your familiar environment. You will be logged in to your own account and all your installed apps will be available.

Let's fire up that simulator and see what it can do. Open up a Windows Store app solution in Visual Studio 2012, and make sure that the app isn't installed on your device. Click the small arrow next to the debug button, as shown in Figure 2-10.

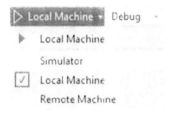

Figure 2-10. *The run options in Visual Studio 2012*

Local Machine is set by default, which means it is deploying and running on your actual machine. Remote Machine means we can run and debug applications on any device with the necessary remote debugging tools installed to which we have access through via a variety of means, for example, our local network. Select the Simulator, click run, and the simulator should fire up and launch the app, as shown in Figure 2-11.

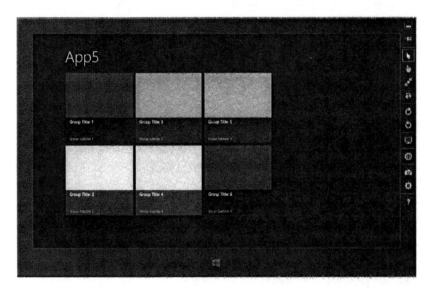

Figure 2-11. *The simulator*

There it is, looking like a tablet. Now to prove that it really hooks into your actual Windows 8 installation, before doing anything else go to the Start menu on your device and scroll all the way back. Notice the app that's running on the simulator? That's right, it's installed on your device.

The simulator allows us to use touch features on a nontouch device. The third and fourth buttons from the top (the arrow and the pointing hand) switch the simulator between mouse and touch capabilities. The fifth button simulates pinch-to-zoom, clicking and holding the left mouse button while using the scroll wheel will give the effect (you can try it on the Start screen in the simulator, just click the button on the bottom side). The seventh and eight buttons rotate the simulator to test if your app rescales to the inverted resolution, as shown in Figure 2-12.

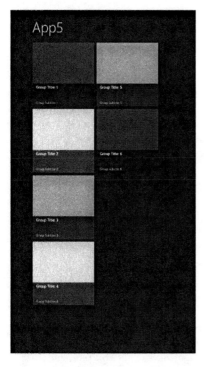

Figure 2-12. *App running in portrait mode*

Allowing your app to adjust according to the dimension of the device gives a great user experience, so please consider implementing it. Even if you don't, rotate the simulator once to make sure your app doesn't crash on it because that will fail the certification.

Equally important to handling rotation is handling different resolutions. The simulator makes it easy to switch resolutions on the fly, as shown in Figure 2-13.

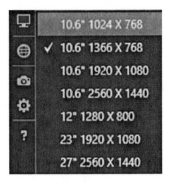

Figure 2-13. *Different screen sizes and resolutions supported by simulator*

By default, the selected resolution is the same one that is set on your physical device. The choices range from the very minimum resolution that allows Windows Store apps to run (1024 × 768, anything lower will just give an error message when trying to run a Windows Store app, including the one started from Visual Studio) to a pretty big 2560 × 1440. Note that besides resolution, the dots per inch (DPI) of a screen also determines how much screen real estate we have for our apps. Many controls in the Windows 8 SDK scale by themselves, a GridView, for example, will show less rows per column on a lower resolution (the Windows 8 Start screen is a great example of this). Make sure to test your app on different resolutions and make them use as much available space as possible. An app that looks great on 1366 × 768 but has two-thirds white space on 1920 × 1080 is not a great user experience, and it's a waste of space.

Summary

In this chapter, we've discussed the different versions of Visual Studio 2012, going from the full-blown versions, such as Ultimate, Premium, and Professional, to the Express edition that has a separate install for each technology, such as Windows Store, Windows Desktop, and Web.

We've also discussed the different templates that are included in the Windows 8 SDK: the Blank Template (an empty screen that requires you to do all the hard work and start completely from scratch); the Grid Template (a three-page template containing a grouped GridView, a group detail page, and an item detail page); and a Split App Template (a two-page template containing a split page that has a list of items and a detail view). The detail view is updated automatically if another item is selected in the list.

In the last part of this chapter, we discussed the simulator, a software device that can emulate touch, multitouch, orientation changes, and resolution changes. I can't stress enough the importance of these features. If you don't own a device that has an accelerometer to detect orientation changes, make sure to test how your app behaves by using this simulator.

In the next chapter we will start our first projects, ready? Let's go!

CHAPTER 3

■ ■ ■

Building a First Project

So far we've taken a look at installing the newest version of Visual Studio, a very exciting new release of what I believe is one of the best integrated development environments out there. We've also gotten a first taste at how it feels to develop and run a Windows Store app, so now it's time to take that feeling to the next level. This chapter will show how to build a complete, good-looking application. We'll add pages to the project and learn how to navigate to those pages and how to pass data between them. We'll also have a look at Model View ViewModel (MVVM), think Model View Controller but for XAML, including a great toolkit that provides an implementation of the MVVM design pattern. And to finish off we'll learn that an important piece of XAML that is very commonly used in Windows Presentation Foundation (WPF), Silverlight, and Windows Phone is missing in Windows RT. But no worries, we'll figure something out.

We're going to build a complete application in this chapter. The application will be a quiz, where the first screen will show some subjects and the player will select a subject and get a multiple choice question with four possible answers. Clicking the correct answer will take the player to a congratulations page, but clicking the wrong answer will show the game over page. Pretty basic, but it contains pages, navigation, and it can be hooked up to an MVVM scenario.

Adding Pages

This chapter will focus on adding pages to a project and building the layout. We'll be discussing GridViews, StackPanels, WrapPanels, and many more.

Let's get started! For this chapter we're going to use the Grid App Template that was discussed in Chapter 2. Select that template, choose a location to store the project, and click OK, as shown in Figure 3-1.

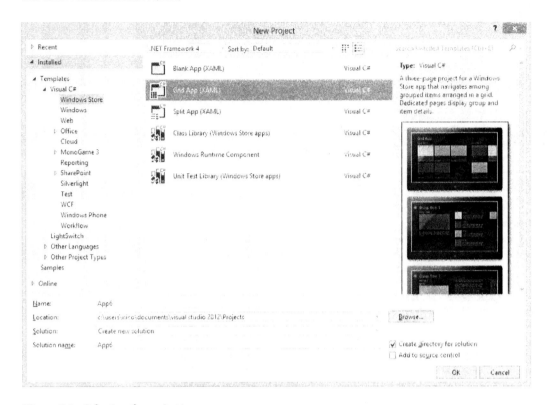

Figure 3-1. *Selecting the project type*

GridView

As mentioned, this template was discussed in the previous chapter. Now let's take a closer look at the controls that are on the page, starting with the GridView, as shown in Listing 3-1.

Listing 3-1. GridView

```
<GridView
            x:Name="itemGridView"
            AutomationProperties.AutomationId="ItemGridView"
            AutomationProperties.Name="Grouped Items"
            Grid.RowSpan="2"
            Padding="116,137,40,46"
            ItemsSource="{Binding Source={StaticResource groupedItemsViewSource}}"
            ItemTemplate="{StaticResource Standard250x250ItemTemplate}"
            SelectionMode="None"
            IsSwipeEnabled="false"
            IsItemClickEnabled="True"
            ItemClick="ItemView_ItemClick">
```

As you can see, the ItemTemplate property of the GridView is bound to a static resource. That resource is included in this template and can be found under the common folder called StandardStyles.xaml, as shown in Listing 3-2.

Listing 3-2. DataTemplate

```
<DataTemplate x:Key="Standard250x250ItemTemplate">
    <Grid HorizontalAlignment="Left" Width="250" Height="250">
        <Border Background="{StaticResource ListViewItemPlaceholderBackgroundThemeBrush}">
            <Image Source="{Binding Image}" Stretch="UniformToFill"
AutomationProperties.Name="{Binding Title}"/>
        </Border>
        <StackPanel VerticalAlignment="Bottom" Background="{StaticResource
ListViewItemOverlayBackgroundThemeBrush}">
            <TextBlock Text="{Binding Title}" Foreground="{StaticResource
ListViewItemOverlayForegroundThemeBrush}" Style="{StaticResource TitleTextStyle}"
Height="60" Margin="15,0,15,0"/>
            <TextBlock Text="{Binding Subtitle}" Foreground="{StaticResource
ListViewItemOverlaySecondaryForegroundThemeBrush}" Style="{StaticResource CaptionTextStyle}"
TextWrapping="NoWrap" Margin="15,0,15,10"/>
        </StackPanel>
    </Grid>
</DataTemplate>
```

This is the template used for the items in the GridView. It's basically a grid that contains an image and some text blocks, which is surrounded by a border. The StackPanel containing the text blocks overlaps the image and is a bit transparent, giving it a nice modern look.

Back to the GridView, there's an event handler attached to the ItemClick event to respond to the user clicking an item.

■ **Note**   When using the ItemClick event, don't forget to set the IsItemClickEnabled property to true or the event won't fire.

The other properties of the GridView will determine how the GridView is drawn on the screen, how or if it wraps the items, and so on, as shown in the code in Listing 3-3 for GroupStyle.

Listing 3-3. GroupStyle

```
<GridView.GroupStyle>
    <GroupStyle>
        <GroupStyle.HeaderTemplate>
            <DataTemplate>
                <Grid Margin="1,0,0,6">
                    <Button
                        AutomationProperties.Name="Group Title"
                        Click="Header_Click"
                        Style="{StaticResource TextPrimaryButtonStyle}" >
                        <StackPanel Orientation="Horizontal">
                            <TextBlock Text="{Binding Title}" Margin="3,-7,10,10"
Style="{StaticResource GroupHeaderTextStyle}" />
                            <TextBlock Text="{StaticResource ChevronGlyph}" FontFamily="Segoe UI
Symbol" Margin="0,-7,0,10" Style="{StaticResource GroupHeaderTextStyle}"/>
                        </StackPanel>
                    </Button>
```

```
                </Grid>
            </DataTemplate>
        </GroupStyle.HeaderTemplate>
        <GroupStyle.Panel>
            <ItemsPanelTemplate>
                <VariableSizedWrapGrid Orientation="Vertical" Margin="0,0,80,0"/>
            </ItemsPanelTemplate>
        </GroupStyle.Panel>
    </GroupStyle>
</GridView.GroupStyle>
```

We'll go over these properties from top to bottom. The first one is the HeaderTemplate, which is mainly used when you're using grouping in the GridView, such as the template does. It's not necessary to do that, and you can build a great GridView that doesn't have any groups at all. Every item, header, or other template consists of a DataTemplate, which then contains all the controls, in this case a button with a style that makes it look just like a text block. In Windows Store app development, your content is your navigation, so the group titles are a perfect way of navigating to other pages of your application.

■ **Note** Try to avoid any buttons on the pages for navigation. Buttons can be placed in the app bars, but they shouldn't be the main way of navigating.

The second template, after the GroupStyle, we encounter in this GridView is the ItemsPanelTemplate. A GridView provides a very basic way of ordering items. If we want we can gain more control over the way items are displayed, and that's where the ItemsPanelTemplate comes in. The DataTemplate we define here is the one that will be used for ordering and displaying the items. It can go from a grid to a stack panel or a VariableSizedWrapGrid in this case. The VariableSizedWrapGrid provides a grid layout where every item can differ in size by making them span multiple rows and columns. This is commonly used to make the first item in the grid stand out from the rest, for example, an important headline in a news reader app. The WrapGrid part of the VariableSizedWrapGrid means that it will automatically wrap items to the next row or column instead of showing scrollbars.

■ **Note** Do not try to set the items in a grid layout, because on a machine with a different resolution, your layout will be messed up. When using a WrapGrid, the control will take care of scaling the items correctly on any resolution.

That's it for the GridView, a pretty easy yet very powerful control that can effectively scale over different resolutions and orientations. The way that the HeaderTemplate and the ItemsPanelTemplate are defined here can also be used to define the ItemTemplate, such as the example in Listing 3-4 shows.

Listing 3-4. ItemTemplate

```
<GridView.ItemTemplate>
    <DataTemplate>
        <Border BorderBrush="Black" BorderThickness="2" Width="300" HorizontalAlignment="Left"
Height="120">
            <StackPanel Orientation="Horizontal" VerticalAlignment="Center" Margin="10,0,0,0">
                <StackPanel>
                    <TextBlock Text="{Binding Name}" Width="180" Foreground="Black"
Margin="12,0,0,0" TextWrapping="Wrap" />
```

```
                        <TextBlock Text="{Binding Url, Converter={StaticResource TextShorter}}"
Width="180" Foreground="Black" Margin="12,0,0,0" TextWrapping="NoWrap" />
                    </StackPanel>
                </StackPanel>
            </Border>
        </DataTemplate>
    </GridView.ItemTemplate>
```

Don't worry too much about those binding and converter statements in there, we'll take a look at those in a minute.

StackPanel

I've mentioned the StackPanel a few times already. Those who've had some experience with XAML, either from WPF, Silverlight, or Windows Phone, will know exactly what that and the other item containers are. For the rest, let's do a quick overview. Don't worry, they are not complex at all and they don't need the same lengthy explanation as the GridView. I will explain those that are more complex as we encounter them.

Let's start with the StackPanel, which orders items either under one another or next to one another. The most important property here is Orientation, which can be either horizontal or vertical, with the default being vertical, as in the example in Listing 3-5.

Listing 3-5. Vertical StackPanel

```
<StackPanel>
    <TextBlock Text="Enter Name" Width="180"  />
    <TextBox Text="{Binding Name}" Width="180" />
</StackPanel>
```

The StackPanel in Listing 3-5 will show a text block and a text box nicely aligned on top of each other. Listing 3-6 shows the code for a horizontal StackPanel.

Listing 3-6. Horizontal StackPanel

```
<StackPanel Orientation="Horizontal">
    <TextBlock Text="Enter Name" Width="180"  />
    <TextBox Text="{Binding Name}" Width="180" />
</StackPanel>
```

This StackPanel will show those same controls side by side. A commonly used scenario for a StackPanel is a form, such as the one presented in Listing 3-7 taken from one of my apps.

Listing 3-7. StackPanel Form

```
<StackPanel x:Name="LayOutPopUp" Margin="342,133,346,208" Height="300" Grid.Row="1"
Grid.ColumnSpan="2" Background="#FFEAE5E5" Visibility="Collapsed">
    <TextBlock TextWrapping="Wrap" Text="Name" Style="{StaticResource BasicTextStyle}"
Margin="10,10,0,0"/>
    <TextBox x:Name="TextBoxName" TextWrapping="Wrap" Margin="10,0"/>
    <TextBlock TextWrapping="Wrap" Text="Url" Margin="10,20,0,0"
Style="{StaticResource BasicTextStyle}"/>
    <TextBox x:Name="TextBoxUrl" TextWrapping="Wrap" Margin="10,0"/>
```

```xml
    <TextBlock TextWrapping="Wrap" Text="Tags, seperated by semicolumns ( ; )"
Margin="10,20,0,0" Style="{StaticResource BasicTextStyle}"/>
    <TextBox x:Name="TextBoxTags" TextWrapping="Wrap" Margin="10,0"/>
    <Grid Margin="0,20,10,20" HorizontalAlignment="Right" Width="658" Height="90">
        <TextBlock x:Name="TextBlockError" TextWrapping="Wrap" Text="You need to fill in all
textboxes to continue" Style="{StaticResource BasicTextStyle}" VerticalAlignment="Center"
Height="27" Foreground="#DEA00D0D" FontWeight="Bold" Margin="121,22,203,41" Visibility="Collapsed"/>
        <StackPanel Height="71" Orientation="Horizontal" HorizontalAlignment="Right"
Width="183" Margin="0,0,0,19">
            <Button Content="Save" HorizontalAlignment="Stretch" VerticalAlignment="Stretch"
Width="80" Click="Button_Click_3"/>
            <Button Content="Cancel" HorizontalAlignment="Stretch"
VerticalAlignment="Stretch" Margin="20,0,0,0" Width="80" Click="Button_Click_2"/>
        </StackPanel>
    </Grid>
</StackPanel>
```

Notice the StackPanel inside the StackPanel in Listing 3-7? That's because all controls are stacked vertically, and we needed two buttons next to each other.

Grid

Another very common container is the Grid. Every page you create in a Windows Store app consists of a Grid by default. This can be changed into any other container control, such as a StackPanel. A Grid can be divided into rows and columns of set or variable sizes, and controls can then be placed into one of those cells or they can be made to span multiple cells. Listing 3-8 presents an example of the Grid.

Listing 3-8. Grid

```xml
<Grid Margin="50,50,10,10" Grid.Row="0" Grid.ColumnSpan="2">
    <Grid.ColumnDefinitions>
        <ColumnDefinition Width="*" />
        <ColumnDefinition Width="*" />
    </Grid.ColumnDefinitions>
    <Grid.RowDefinitions>
        <RowDefinition Height="Auto" />
        <RowDefinition Height="*" />
    </Grid.RowDefinitions>
        <TextBlock Grid.Row="0" Grid.Column="1" Foreground="Gray" FontFamily="Segoe UI Light"
FontSize="45" Text="Developer links" />
</Grid>
```

This Grid contains two rows and two columns. The two columns each have half of the Grid's width. The size of the rows and columns can either be set by using an absolute size (in pixels), by using the star notation (space needed by the controls), or a combination of both. The first row will size automatically based on what's inside that row, and the second row will have all the remaining space. The text block that is in the Grid is set to the first row and the second column, and the rows' and columns' indices are zero based, meaning that the first row or column has index 0. These are called *attached properties* because they are properties from a parent control that attach themselves to a child control.

Canvas

Another container that is commonly used is the Canvas, which is typically used for absolute positioning of controls operations page. This can be a big disadvantage when dealing with different resolutions and screen sizes. An example of the code for the Canvas is shown in Listing 3-9.

Listing 3-9. Canvas

```
<Canvas Width="640" Height="480" Background="White">
    <Rectangle Canvas.Left="30" Canvas.Top="30"
               Fill="red" Width="200" Height="200" />
</Canvas>
```

No matter where on the page this canvas is drawn or what the resolution of the device is, the rectangle inside the Canvas will always be drawn at 30 pixels from the top and 30 pixels from the left of the Canvas. This kind of functionality makes the Canvas a great element for games built in XAML.

■ **Note** The Canvas element has some similarities to the HTML5 Canvas element. They share some of the same features and advantages.

The Grid, the StackPanel, and the Canvas are the most common XAML controls that are used to lay out a page in an XAML project. That's why I spent some time on that here. We'll take a closer look at other controls throughout this book.

Our Project

All right, all very interesting stuff. Now back to our little project. The GroupDetailPage has basically the same layout as the first page. The big difference here is the HeaderTemplate, as shown in Listing 3-10.

Listing 3-10. GridView

```
<GridView.Header>
    <StackPanel Width="480" Margin="0,4,14,0">
        <TextBlock Text="{Binding Subtitle}" Margin="0,0,18,20"
Style="{StaticResource SubheaderTextStyle}" MaxHeight="60"/>
        <Image Source="{Binding Image}" Height="400" Margin="0,0,18,20"
Stretch="UniformToFill" AutomationProperties.Name="{Binding Title}"/>
        <TextBlock Text="{Binding Description}" Margin="0,0,18,0"
Style="{StaticResource BodyTextStyle}"/>
    </StackPanel>
</GridView.Header>
```

This header spans the entire height of the GridView, giving the illusion that the first group in the Grid has another template. Other than that, there's not really any difference between the two pages in the project.

Adding a Page

That second page is pretty useless to us for the moment. Let's add a new page that we'll use to ask the quiz question. Right-click the project in the Solution Explorer and select Add ➤ New Item, as shown in Figure 3-2.

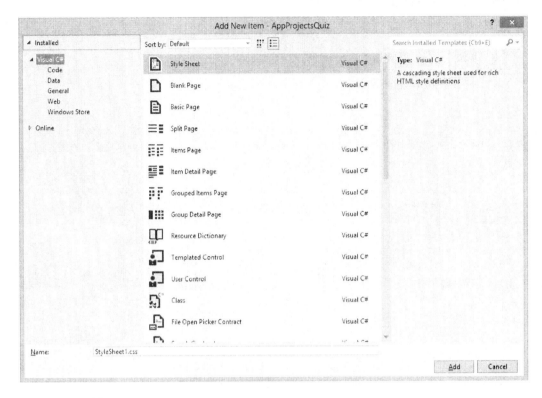

Figure 3-2. *Adding a page*

All the page templates here are the same pages that exist in the project templates for Windows Store apps. We're going to go with the Basic Page for now. The Basic Page inherits from the LayoutAwarePage class and provides all the logic for navigating back, showing a page title with all margins set like the Windows Store guidelines describe, so that's a really good starting point.

■ **Note**   When adding a basic page to a blank project, you might see a dialog box pop up asking you if it's okay to add some stuff to the project. The stuff that it wants to add is everything found in the Common folder, such as the LayoutAwarePage class and StandarStyles.xaml. We'll get back to those in more detail later in the book.

So we've taken a look at the most commonly used item containers and we've added a page to our project. What we're going to do next is clean up the project a bit and start adding some navigation and a basic layout to it.

Let's start by adding another new page to the project called MainPage. Next we'll remove all pages except for the two pages we've added ourselves. So remove GroupDetailPage, GroupedItemsPage, and ItemDetailPage. Now when we try to build the solution, it will throw a build error stating that *GroupedItemsPage could not be found.*

That's because that page is set to launch when the application starts, so let's change that. Open `App.xaml.cs`, navigate to the `OnLaunched` method, and find this part of the code:

```
if (!rootFrame.Navigate(typeof(GroupedItemsPage), "AllGroups"))
{
    throw new Exception("Failed to create initial page");
}
```

This is the piece of code that initializes and shows the first page of the application. Replace the `typeof(GroupedItemsPage)` with `typeof(MainPage)` and our app should run fine again, although it will no longer show any items. We could've just started off with a blank project and started adding items, but then I wouldn't have been able to explain the `GridView` properly.

Let's get our `MainPage` to show some items that navigate to another page when clicked. First, we're going to need to set the `DataContext` of that page. The `DataContext` is an instance of a class where the controls that are bound will look for their source. To start, we're going to bind to properties that are in the code behind the page. To do that, we set the `DataContext` at the top of the `MainPage.xaml`, as shown here:

```
DataContext="{Binding RelativeSource={RelativeSource Self}}"
```

Next, we'll create a data source to retrieve some data. We'll take a look at contacting services later in the book, so for this example I have some hard-coded data. In `MainPage.xaml`, we'll retrieve all subjects and show them in a GridView. I prefer to retrieve the data from the `OnNavigatedTo` event instead of from the constructor as the constructor isn't always called when navigating to this page because when we navigate back to a page we go back to the existing instance. First, declare a property to contain all the subjects, then call the data source to load the subjects, as shown in Listing 3-11.

Listing 3-11. OnNavigatedTo Method

```
public List<string> Subjects { get; set; }

protected override void OnNavigatedTo(NavigationEventArgs e)
{
        Subjects = QuizDataSource.GetSubjects();

        base.OnNavigatedTo(e);
}
```

When overriding the `OnNavigatedTo` event handler, don't forget to call the base `OnNavigatedTo` method. If you forget this, the app will crash whenever a user clicks the Back button to navigate back to this page. That's because this page inherits from the `LayoutAwarePage` base class. The `OnNavigatedTo` method in that base class configures the `SuspensionManager`, so we can easily navigate back to this page.

Now add a GridView to the page and bind its ItemsSource to the `Subjects` property, as demonstrated in Listing 3-12.

Listing 3-12. GridView with ItemsSource

```
<GridView Grid.Row="1" Margin="120,0,0,0"
        ItemsSource="{Binding Subjects}">

</GridView>
```

When we run the app now it should look like the example shown in Figure 3-3.

Figure 3-3. *Our app*

Our binding seems to be working, good work! Time to add some navigation. First, we need the GridView to respond to an item click, as demonstrated in Listing 3-13.

Listing 3-13. GridView with Properties

```
<GridView Grid.Row="1" Margin="120,0,0,0"
          ItemsSource="{Binding Subjects}"
          IsItemClickEnabled="True"
          ItemClick="GridView_ItemClick_1">

</GridView>
```

Don't forget to set the IsItemClickEnabled property to true or your grid won't respond to the ItemClick event. Listing 3-14 shows how we navigate to the next page.

Listing 3-14. Navigation

```
private void GridView_ItemClick_1(object sender, ItemClickEventArgs e)
{
    Frame.Navigate(typeof (QuizPage));
}
```

Every XAML-based app consists of a frame that shows the necessary page. The `Navigate` method takes the page that's passed as a parameter and displays it in the frame. In Windows Phone apps, the page was passed as a string, and in Windows Store apps, it's passed as a type. The biggest advantage we have in this is IntelliSense support and less chance of runtime errors for our users. With that in place, our app should navigate to our second page when an item in the GridView is clicked.

Navigating is one thing but it could also come in handy to pass some data from one page to the next. The `Navigate` method has an overload that allows data to pass through to the next page. The parameter is of type object so basically we can pass anything. For our quiz application we'll pass the subject, so here just a string. Modify the `Frame.Navigate` call to look like this:

```
Frame.Navigate(typeof (QuizPage), e.ClickedItem);
```

QuizPage

On to our QuizPage we go. On this page we need to overwrite the `OnNavigatedTo` method just like we did on the `MainPage`. The `NavigationEventArgs` that gets passed into the `OnNavigatedTo` method has the parameter that we passed in the navigation call. We're going to take that parameter and set it to a property that we can then bind to the page title, as shown in Listing 3-15.

Listing 3-15. Title Property

```
public string Title { get; set; }

protected override void OnNavigatedTo(NavigationEventArgs e)
{
    if(e.Parameter != null)
    {
        Title = e.Parameter.ToString();
    }

    base.OnNavigatedTo(e);
}
```

We first check to see if there actually is a parameter, and if there is, we pass it to the `Title` property. Second, we need to adjust the title `TextBlock` in the XAML to be bound to the `Title` property, as shown in Listing 3-16.

Listing 3-16. Bound TextBlock

```
<TextBlock x:Name="pageTitle" Grid.Column="1" Text="{Binding Title}" Style="{StaticResource
PageHeaderTextStyle}"/>
```

Don't forget to set the correct `DataContext` for the page or there won't be any title showing. Run the app, click a subject, and see the power of data binding hard at work. Cool stuff right? Well, if you like this, you'll love what comes next.

MVVM and MVVM Light

Model View ViewModel (MVVM) is a design pattern that describes a way of separating the business logic from the view, making it easy to write unit tests for an app. It also makes it really easy when your team has a designer and a developer, as the designer doesn't need to worry about code at all. But the most important advantage of MVVM is the fact that it forces the developers to use the data-binding framework and all the advantages that come with it. It's all about relaying responsibility from one component to another component in order to get a better separation of concerns, which in turn results in better testability. The MVVM structure is presented in Figure 3-4.

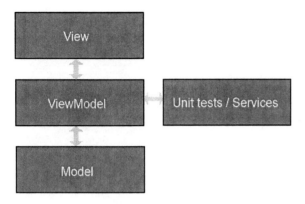

Figure 3-4. *The MVVM structure*

As you can see in Figure 3-4, the view knows about the ViewModel and the ViewModel knows about the model. The view has no idea where data come from and doesn't need to know, just like the model has no idea who is showing the data. Try to avoid writing any code behind a page as it can break the testability of your project.

MVVM has a lot of advantages, but it can be kind of a drag to set everything up. There are many frameworks and toolkits that provide a lot of that boiler plate code and help you get started quickly. A very popular one that I tend to use quite often is the open source toolkit MVVM Light by Laurent Bugnion. MVVM Light provides a ViewModelBase so we don't have to implement INotifyPropertyChanged anymore (implementation sits in the ViewModelBase), an inversion of control (IoC) container, a messenger, a ViewModel locator, and a bunch of code snippets that we can use while developing apps. All that combined makes for an extensive and easy-to-use MVVM toolkit. Let's walk through converting our conventional app into an MVVM-driven application.

Getting Started with MVVM Light

There are different ways of building an MVVM Light application. The easiest way is to use the installer that can be found on the project's home page. That installer adds a few Visual Studio templates and installs a bunch of snippets. If you want to convert an existing application to MVVM Light or you don't want to install everything, there's always good old NuGet. Use NuGet now to add the MVVM Light binaries to the project, as shown in Figure 3-5.

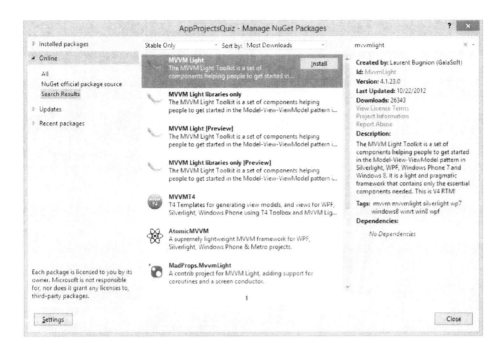

Figure 3-5. *Getting MVVM Light through NuGet*

Installing this NuGet package will perform some tasks with your project, such as adding a folder that holds the ViewModels and the ViewModelLocator. The folder structure makes it easier for developers to find the code files we need when the code gets bigger. Figure 3-6 shows the tree as it looks before using MVVM Light. Figure 3-7 shows the tree after applying MVVM Light.

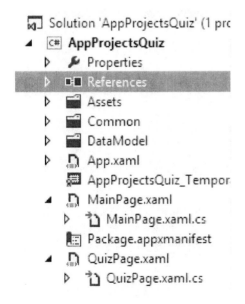

Figure 3-6. *Before MVVM Light*

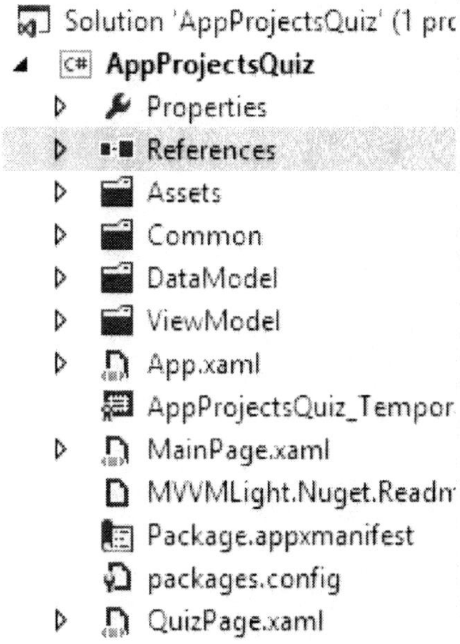

Solution 'AppProjectsQuiz' (1 pro
▲ C# **AppProjectsQuiz**
  ▷ 🔧 Properties
  ▷ ▪▪ References
  ▷ 📁 Assets
  ▷ 📁 Common
  ▷ 📁 DataModel
  ▷ 📁 ViewModel
  ▷ 🗋 App.xaml
     📄 AppProjectsQuiz_Tempor
  ▷ 🗋 MainPage.xaml
     🗋 MVVMLight.Nuget.Readm
     🗋 Package.appxmanifest
     🗋 packages.config
  ▷ 🗋 QuizPage.xaml

Figure 3-7. *After MVVM Light*

At the time of writing, there was a small issue with MVVM Light in Windows Store apps. When we tried to build the application after adding MVVM Light, we would get this build error:

```
Unknown type 'ViewModelLocator' in XML namespace 'clr-namespace:AppProjectsQuiz.ViewModel;
assembly=AppProjectsQuiz, Version=1.0.0.0, Culture=neutral, PublicKeyToken=null'
```

This is easily fixed though. In the `App.xaml` file, search for this piece of code in the namespace declarations:

```
xmlns:vm="clr-namespace:AppProjectsQuiz.ViewModel"
```

Replace it with:

```
xmlns:vm="Using:AppProjectsQuiz.ViewModel"
```

That should suffice to build the application, and it should still run and function as it did before we added the MVVM Light libraries.

ViewModelLocator

The ViewModelLocator is where everything gets hooked up. It registers the IoC container of your choice (or the built-in `SimpleIoC` class), and it registers ViewModels so that their properties can be used for binding on the View. The `ViewModelLocator` class can be found in the `ViewModel` folder. Listing 3-17 shows what the class should look like.

Listing 3-17. ViewModelLocator

```
public class ViewModelLocator
{
    /// <summary>
    /// Initializes a new instance of the ViewModelLocator class.
    /// </summary>
    public ViewModelLocator()
    {
        ServiceLocator.SetLocatorProvider(() => SimpleIoc.Default);
        SimpleIoc.Default.Register<MainViewModel>();
    }

    public MainViewModel Main
    {
        get
        {
            return ServiceLocator.Current.GetInstance<MainViewModel>();
        }
    }

    public static void Cleanup()
    {
        // TODO Clear the ViewModels
    }
}
```

In the ViewModelLocator, we need to create a property for each ViewModel we want to use. That model gets instantiated and registered into the IoC container. An IoC container is an object that contains many registered classes. Whenever a class in a project has a dependency on one of these registered classes, we can use the IoC to inject the dependency into the class. Let me clarify with an example. Let's say we have the code in Listing 3-18.

Listing 3-18. Example Without IoC

```
Private SqlDataService service;
Public MyClass()
{
    service = new SqlDataService();
}
```

What you see here is a class called MyClass that has a dependency on SqlDataService, meaning MyClass knows what class is getting the data and where it gets them. There is nothing wrong with this at first sight, but what if the customer decides to go from SqlDataService to RestDataService? We would need to change MyClass and all other dependencies. Listing 3-19 shows the same code but with dependency injection (DI).

Listing 3-19. Example with IoC and DI

```
Private IDataService service;
Public MyClass(IDataService dataService)
{
    service = dataService;
}
```

In this code, the IDataService is an interface, meaning that we can inject any class here that implements that interface. The injection happens through the constructor. When it's called, it will search the IoC container for a class that implements IDataService and it will inject that instance into the constructor of MyClass.

■ **Note** MVVM Light uses SimpleIOC by default, which is an open source, very basic, but fast and reliable IoC solution. Should you want to replace it with AutoFAC or any other IoC, it's really easy to do. Just register every ViewModel in the ViewModelLocator and you're good to go.

ViewModels

In the ViewModel folder, there should also be a MainViewModel class, as shown in Listing 3-20.

Listing 3-20. MainViewModel

```
public class MainViewModel : ViewModelBase
{
    /// <summary>
    /// Initializes a new instance of the MainViewModel class.
    /// </summary>
    public MainViewModel()
    {

    }
}
```

Notice that the ViewModel inherits from ViewModelBase. That's just MVVM Light saving us from writing boiler plate code over and over again. The ViewModelBase is an observable abstract class that inherits from ObservableObject, which in turn implements INotifyPropertyChanged, meaning that all our ViewModels that inherit from ViewModelBase can notify their views that properties have changed, as shown in Listing 3-21.

Listing 3-21. ViewModelBase

```
public abstract class ViewModelBase : ObservableObject, ICleanup
{
    ...
}
```

Next to being observable, the ViewModelBase also has a Messenger property that can be set in a constructor overload, eliminating the need to instantiate the messenger in every ViewModel when you're not using the static app-wide instance. Basically, the biggest advantage we get from the ViewModelBase is that we don't need to implement INotifyPropertyChanged for every ViewModel.

Let's start moving code from the view behind to the MainViewModel. We'll start with the list that contains all the subjects.

Remove the Subjects property from the MainPage.xaml.cs and the OnNavigatedTo method needs be removed. Adjust the MainViewModel to look like the example in Listing 3-22.

Listing 3-22. MainViewModel

```
public class MainViewModel : ViewModelBase
{
    private ObservableCollection<string> _subjects;
    public ObservableCollection<string> Subjects
    {
      get { return _subjects; }
      set
      {
          if (_subjects == value) return;

          _subjects = value;
          RaisePropertyChanged(() => Subjects);
      }
    }

    /// <summary>
    /// Initializes a new instance of the MainViewModel class.
    /// </summary>
    public MainViewModel()
    {
        Subjects = QuizDataSource.GetSubjects();
    }
}
```

The first thing we need is a property of type ObservableCollection<T> and a call to the data store to fill that list. As you can see in Listing 3-22, the Subjects property calls RaisePropertyChanged() from its setter. That function resides in the ViewModelBase and is part of the INotifyPropertyChanged implementation. What it does is notify all controls bound to the Subjects property that the value has changed and that the bindings should refresh. The app should run fine now but won't show any data. That's because we haven't updated our bindings. The MainPage goes searching for the Subjects property in its code behind the file. Remember the DataContext statement in the MainPage.xaml? Change it to point to the MainViewModel, as shown in the code:

```
DataContext="{Binding Main, Source={StaticResource Locator}}"
```

We set it to bind to Main, that's the name we gave to the property of type MainViewModel in the ViewModelLocator. We also need to set the source so the app will know where to look. The source is the ViewModelLocator, which gets instantiated by making it available as a resource in App.xaml. The getter for Main resolves the MainViewModel instance in the SimpleIOC container and returns that. The result is that whenever we go to the MainPage, we always get the same instance in this implementation, or you could choose to get a new instance every time. That could come in handy when dealing with a data-intensive app. Just remember to trigger a data refresh if it is needed. Run the application again and the list of subjects should show up again. Even the navigation still works, although that's still being handled in the code behind.

Note There are lots of discussions whether or not page navigation can be put in the code behind the pages. It's up to you whether you do it or not, I'm just going to put everything in the ViewModels here just to show you how it can be done.

Navigation in MVVM

There are different ways of handling navigation in an MVVM scenario. I'm going to explain the one that I tend to use because I find it easy to understand and use. I have an INavigationService interface that comes from my Windows Phone projects. Using this interface makes it easier to port my applications between both platforms. That interface is shown in the example in Listing 3-23.

Listing 3-23. Navigation Interface

```
public interface INavigationService
{
    bool CanGoBack { get; }
    bool CanGoForward { get; }
    void GoBack();
    void GoForward();
    void Initialize(global::Windows.UI.Xaml.Window window, bool activate = true);
    void Navigate(Type destination, object parameter = null);
}
```

It has the same properties and methods as the Frame class, which makes it easy to copy our existing code over. Let's take a look at the implementation of this interface, as shown in Listing 3-24.

Listing 3-24. Interface Implementation

```
public class NavigationService : INavigationService
{
    public void Initialize(Window window, bool activate = true)
    {
        if (window.Content == null)
            window.Content = App.RootFrame;

        if (activate)
            window.Activate();
    }

    public virtual void Navigate(Type destination, object parameter = null)
    {
        // avoid navigation if current equals to destination

        if (App.RootFrame.CurrentSourcePageType != destination)
            App.RootFrame.Navigate(destination, parameter);
    }

    public virtual void GoBack()
    {
        if (App.RootFrame.CanGoBack)
            App.RootFrame.GoBack();
    }
```

```
    public virtual void GoForward()
    {
        if (App.RootFrame.CanGoForward)
            App.RootFrame.GoForward();
    }

    public virtual bool CanGoBack
    {
        get { return App.RootFrame.CanGoBack; }
    }

    public virtual bool CanGoForward
    {
        get { return App.RootFrame.CanGoForward; }
    }
}
```

The Initialize method checks if the active window has an active Frame, if it doesn't it takes the RootFrame property from the App class and sets it as active. The Navigate method works exactly the same way as Frame.Navigate, so we can pass in a class name to navigate to and, optionally, a parameter. The GoBack and GoForward methods navigate the navigation stack, while the two Booleans—CanGoBack and CanGoForward—determine if we're at the beginning or the end of the stack. Now, where did that RootFrame property come from? It's something we need to add to App.xaml.cs because that currently is the only place in an application to set some app-wide content. It is possible to add other container classes for app-wide content, but that would require some architectural changes, which goes beyond the scope of this book.

RootFrame is a pretty easy property to explain. It just returns the Window content cast as a Frame, as demonstrated in Listing 3-25.

Listing 3-25. RootFrame Property

```
public static Frame RootFrame
{
    get { return (Frame)Window.Current.Content; }
}
```

This should do the trick. Now we need to get this class instantiated and passed around in our app, luckily we already have an IoC container in place, which will be very willing to take care of this for us. In the ViewModelLocator add this code in the constructor:

```
if (!ViewModelBase.IsInDesignModeStatic)
{
    SimpleIoc.Default.Register<INavigationService, NavigationService>();
}
```

What's this all about? Well, when we open a page in design mode, either in Visual Studio 2012 or in Blend 5, the code behind that page gets executed. In our case, it will try to register a NavigationService instance. But that class only works at runtime, so the designer will throw an error. By checking if we're running in design mode, we can fix this error. When we're at runtime, we will register type INavigationService and bound to that will be an instance of NavigationService.

So we've got a NavigationService that is registered in our IoC container. Now we need to resolve that instance in our view models. That couldn't actually be any easier—just add a parameter to the constructor of the view model where you want to use the navigation, as shown in Listing 3-26.

Listing 3-26. MainViewModel

```
private INavigationService _navigationService;

public MainViewModel(INavigationService navigationService)
{
    _navigationService = navigationService;
    Subjects = QuizDataSource.GetSubjects();
}
```

Now when we run the app, the IoC container should "automagically" resolve the INavigationService instance, as shown in Figure 3-8.

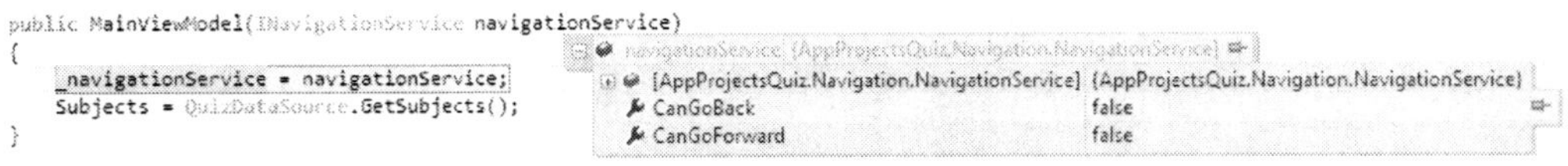

Figure 3-8. *IoC working its magic*

Okay we're almost there. Now we need to find a way to hook the item clicked event to a method in the ViewModel. That's what the ICommand interface is for. Laurent Bugnion was kind enough to provide an implementation in MVVM Light called RelayCommand. There's only one problem, we can't bind the ItemClicked event from the GridView to a RelayCommand. So that's a no-go. Another way is to add a new property to the ViewModel and bind the GridView's SelectedItem property to it, then in the setting of that property we can handle the navigation, as shown in Listing 3-27.

Listing 3-27. The New Property

```
private string _selectedSubject;
public string SelectedSubject
{
    get { return _selectedSubject; }
    set
  {
      If(_selectedSubject == value) return;

        _selectedSubject = value;

        _navigationService.Navigate(typeof(QuizPage), _selectedSubject);
    }
}
```

Next we need to adjust the bindings on the GridView:

```
<GridView Grid.Row="1" Margin="120,0,0,0"
          ItemsSource="{Binding Subjects}"
          IsItemClickEnabled="False"
          SelectedItem="{Binding SelectedSubject, Mode=TwoWay}">

</GridView>
```

IsItemClickEnabled is set to False this time because we aren't actually clicking an item, but rather selecting one. Next, the SelectedItem property is bound to the property on the ViewModel. Don't forget to set the Mode to TwoWay because we want the view to update the ViewModel rather than the other way around. That's it! We're now navigating in an MVVM scenario, good job!

Where Are My Behaviors?

If you've ever done XAML development, you've heard about behaviors. *Behaviors* are reusable pieces of code that can get executed when an event fires or when some other action occurs. This can be useful in an MVVM scenario to bind certain user interface interactions, like clicking a button, to an action in the ViewModel rather than in the code behind the file. They are particularly handy when you need to work against a sealed class, if you want to build a framework or library to distribute, or when you want to execute the same action on different events.

You might have been looking for behaviors in Windows RT, but you can stop the search. They just don't exist. For some reason Microsoft decided that it's not necessary to include them in the framework. But community wouldn't be community if they had not fixed that, so Joost Van Schaik, a Dutch Windows Phone MVP, started writing his own WinRT behaviors library. It's on the CodePlex web site and can be installed from NuGet, as shown in Figure 3-9.

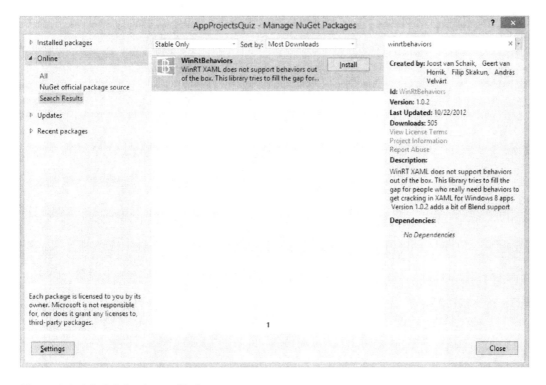

Figure 3-9. *WinRtBehaviors on NuGet*

These should work quite similar to the behaviors found in Windows Phone (for more information check out Joost's blog post on his behaviors at `http://dotnetbyexample.blogspot.be/2012/03/attached-behaviors-for-windows-8-metro.html`).

Summary

This chapter started us into building our first real application. We've added a basic page to the project and a page that contains navigation logic in its base class, `LayoutAwarePage`. We've responded to the `ItemClick` event to navigate to a second page and passed data as a parameter to that second page. We then transformed our application into an MVVM-based scenario using the MVVM Light library. We used the built-in SimpleIoC to register our ViewModels and navigation service. Finally, the absence of behaviors in the WinRT framework was discussed.

In the next chapter we will look at how to handle data.

CHAPTER 4

Consuming Data

An application would be nothing without data. Those data can come from a number of different sources, ranging from a local database, XML or JSON (JavaScript Object Notation) files to a database in the Cloud, or a REST (representational state transfer) service. Windows Store applications allow us to use a range of data stores, although the focus lies mostly on Cloud-connected apps. Although the local database of choice was SQL compact edition in Windows Phone 7, it's now the open source SQLite in Windows 8 and Windows Phone 8. As far as services are concerned, we can target WCF services, sockets, RSS, oData, REST services, and so on. I advise you to choose the method you're most familiar with, but do keep in mind that some constraints might apply in Windows Store apps. Take WCF, for example, it is supported in the Windows Store but it doesn't support all the bindings. Only BasicHttpbinding, NetTcpBinding, NetHttpBinding, and CustomBinding are supported. Since it's perfectly possible to write an entire book on data services, I will focus on the most common and most popular ways of building a service in this chapter.

As mentioned, Microsoft is really pushing app developers toward Cloud-driven apps, which has a few advantages. A Cloud-driven app that goes multiplatform provides the same data for the users across all platforms, delivering a great experience in, for example, an app where you can keep track of a collection. Part of Microsoft's strategy in convincing developers to use the Cloud is making it really easy to create services in the Cloud. That strategy currently consists of two parts. First, there's ASP.NET web application programming interface (API), the successor of WCF web API. A web API lets us create a REST service in the same way we create ASP.NET Model-View-Controller (MVC) applications, so if you have experience there, you're basically good to go! We'll dive into web API a bit further in this chapter. The second part of the strategy in opening up the Cloud to every developer is Windows Azure Mobile Services. In short, create a service, build the tables and columns of a database, and download a Windows Store solution that's hooked up to that service. A mobile service can then be expanded by adding authentication or by changing the server side scripts, all from within the Azure management portal.

The biggest downside of Cloud connecting an app is obviously the cost, and you might have to put in extra time to make the app work offline and to synchronize it to your service, but that depends on the type of app you're building. A lot of app developers are doing this in their free time, so the cost comes out of their own pockets. But before turning away from the Cloud, let's look at the facts. Windows 8 is anticipating around 600 million users in about one or two years after release, and that's a huge market. A lot of these users won't mind paying a few dollars for a great app, or they don't mind some advertising in the apps. I believe that the best way to monetize your app is by making it free with ads and providing an in-app purchase to get rid of the advertisements. Also, the Windows Azure mobile services can hook into Windows 8, Windows Phone, and iOS apps (as of the time of writing). That is a huge potential market. I'm not saying everyone can get rich by developing apps, that's only for the lucky few, but I believe that everyone can at least earn the cost of their Cloud account back.

SQLite in Windows 8

SQLite can best be described as the open source counterpart of SQL compact edition (SQL CE). What's special about SQLite is the fact that it doesn't need an installation of SQL Server. All that's needed are the binaries included in the project. Once that's okay, we can generate a database and use all our relational database skills.

Creating a Basic SQLite App

Let's build an app powered by a local SQLite database. The app that we're going to build is one that I designed with my wife. She works in kindergarten and needed an app to keep track of the observations of the children in her group. So the app itself will allow you to add children's names to the database and add an observation for every child. It's a pretty basic CRUD (create, read, update, delete) app, so let's get hacking.

Before we start pounding away at our keyboards spitting out all kinds of code, we need the SQLite software development kit (SDK). The installers can be found at http://www.sqlite.org/download.html, where you can see that SQLite exists for a number of platforms. Currently, the latest addition is Windows Phone 8 support, so porting one of our apps to the Redmond-built smartphone operating system has gotten even easier. Download and install the Precompiled Binaries for Windows Runtime (it should be a VSIX file).

I saw a question from a fellow Windows Store app dev on Twitter a while ago asking how he could create a new Windows Store project from a blank template with the LayoutAwarePage template included. This is actually quite easy. You would start a new project from the Blank template and remove the MainPage.xaml and MainPage.xaml.cs. You would then add a new page from the Basic template and name it MainPage.xaml. Visual Studio will give you a message saying that it's missing some files and ask if it should add them. You would click Yes and you will have a complete common folder with the LayoutAwarePage and the StandardStyles dictionary.

■ **Note** The StandardStyles dictionary houses all app bar button styles, most of them are commented out. Uncomment those you need, but leave the rest commented out. If you don't, they will get loaded into your visual tree and impact your performance.

So we now should have a basic project to start from. Let's start by adding the SQLite SDK to the project. Right-click the project and select Add Reference. In the Reference Manager, select Windows ➤ Extensions in the left column. From that list check the SQLite for Windows Runtime and the Microsoft Visual C++ Runtime Package, as shown in Figure 4-1. The Visual C++ runtime package is not required to make the app run and use SQLite, but since SQLite is a C++ library, the reference to the Visual C++ Runtime Package is required by the Windows Store. I know from experience that they will fail your app certification if this reference is not included (the Windows App Certification Kit won't pass either, more on this in Chapter 11).

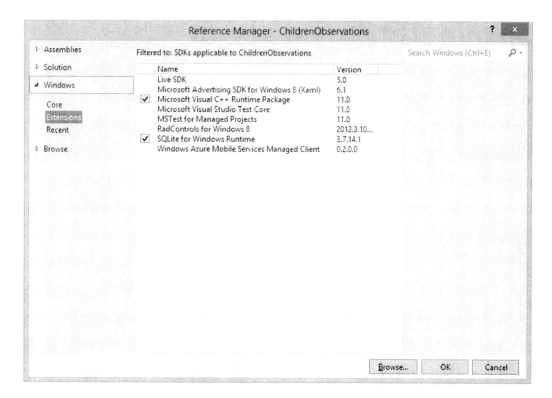

Figure 4-1. *Reference the SQLite libraries*

We now have everything we need to start creating and using SQLite databases to our Windows Store application. However, it would be great if we had a NET wrapper around the SQLite library. Luckily, there's one available on NuGet called sqlite-net, so you can find it and add it to the project. Sqlite-net is actually a real NET project, but it has nothing exotic and no reflection, so it works great in Windows Store apps as well. Do a quick build to see if everything checks out, and let's write some code.

Adding the Child and Observation Classes

We'll begin by creating some classes that will reflect the look of the tables in the database. I have the habit of placing all those classes in a Model folder in the project to keep things clean and easy to navigate. I tend to call this folder Model because it contains my object model, in this case Child and Observation. In this app we'll need two classes: Child and Observation, as provided in Listing 4-1.

Listing 4-1. Observation Class

```
[Table("Observation")]
public class Observation : INotifyPropertyChanged
{
    private string _childName;

    [PrimaryKey, AutoIncrement]
    public int Id { get; set; }
    public int ChildId { get; set; }
```

```
    public string Text { get; set; }
    public DateTime Date { get; set; }

    [Ignore]
    public string ChildName
    {
        get { return _childName; }
        set
        {
            _childName = value;

            OnPropertyChanged("ChildName");
        }
    }

    public event PropertyChangedEventHandler PropertyChanged;

    protected virtual void OnPropertyChanged(string propertyName)
    {
        PropertyChangedEventHandler handler = PropertyChanged;
        if (handler != null) handler(this, new PropertyChangedEventArgs(propertyName));
    }
}
```

The attributes are coming from the SQLite namespace, so don't forget to put that in a using statement.

The Table attribute marks this class as a table, and the parameter is the table name as it will be set in the database. The attributes on the ID property set that property as the primary key with an autoincrement handled by the database. The last attribute found here makes sure that the ChildName property is not used to create a column in the Observation table. Let's take a look at the Child class next, as demonstrated in Listing 4-2.

Listing 4-2. Child Class

```
[Table("Child")]
public class Child
{
    [PrimaryKey, AutoIncrement]
    public int Id { get; set; }
    public string Firstname { get; set; }
    public string Lastname { get; set; }

    [Ignore]
    public string FullName { get { return Firstname + " " + Lastname; } }
}
```

There are very similar attributes in this class as there are in the Observation class, so we move along.

Building the Database and Its Connection

Let's start building that database. We'll start in App.xaml.cs and create a public static property of type SQLiteAsyncConnection:

```
public static SQLiteAsyncConnection Connection { get; set; }
```

Next, in the OnLaunched event, we will try to open a connection to the database. SQLite databases, just like SQL CE databases, are file based, meaning that if the database we try to reach doesn't exist yet, it will throw a FileNotFoundException. Catching that allows us to create a database if it doesn't exist and open one if it does exist, as demonstrated in Listing 4-3.

Listing 4-3. Check if the Database Exists

```
try
{
    await ApplicationData.Current.LocalFolder.GetFileAsync("observations.db");
    Connection = new SQLiteAsyncConnection("observations.db");
}
catch (FileNotFoundException)
{
    CreateDB();
}
```

And the code in Listing 4-4 is used to create a database.

Listing 4-4. Create the Database

```
private async void CreateDB()
{
    Connection = new SQLiteAsyncConnection("observations.db");

    await Connection.CreateTableAsync<Child>();
    await Connection.CreateTableAsync<Observation>();
}
```

You might ask why we put the code to create the database in a separate method. This is because the creation of the tables is done asynchronously and an `await` keyword cannot appear in a `catch` block.

App Functionality

Now on to the app functionality itself. I want the MainPage to display all children, and when I select one, I want to be able to enter an observation for that particular child.

MainPage

We'll start at `MainPage.xaml`. The `DataContext` of `MainPage` is set to itself like this:

```
DataContext="{Binding RelativeSource={RelativeSource Self}}"
```

On the page, we have a GridView that shows all children, derived from the code in Listing 4-5.

Listing 4-5. GridView

```
<GridView HorizontalAlignment="Left" ItemClick="GridView_ItemClick_1" IsItemClickEnabled="True"
Margin="121,10,0,0" Grid.Row="1" ItemsSource="{Binding Children}" VerticalAlignment="Top"
Width="1235" Height="608">
    <GridView.ItemTemplate>
```

```
            <DataTemplate>
                <Border BorderBrush="White">
                    <TextBlock Text="{Binding FullName}" TextWrapping="Wrap" />
                </Border>
            </DataTemplate>
        </GridView.ItemTemplate>
</GridView>
```

As you can see, the items will display as simple text blocks and respond to the item click event of the GridView. The GridView's ItemsSource is bound to the Children collection that is defined in the code behind, as shown in Listing 4-6.

Listing 4-6. Collection Property to Hold All Children

```
private List<Child> _children;
public List<Child> Children
{
    get { return _children; }
    set
    {
        if (_children == value) return;

        _children = value;

        OnPropertyChanged("Children");
    }
}
```

This is just a simple List of type Child. In the item click event handler, we will navigate to the ObservationPage to add a new observation, and as a parameter we'll pass the Child object that was clicked, as demonstrated in Listing 4-7.

Listing 4-7. Selecting a Child

```
private void GridView_ItemClick_1(object sender, ItemClickEventArgs e)
{
    Frame.Navigate(typeof(ObservationPage), e.ClickedItem);
}
```

Observation Page

The observation page consists of a StackPanel with a text block and a textbox, as demonstrated in Listing 4-8.

Listing 4-8. StackPanel on Observation Page

```
<StackPanel HorizontalAlignment="Left" Height="498" Margin="124,10,0,0" Grid.Row="1"
VerticalAlignment="Top" Width="1232">
    <TextBlock TextWrapping="Wrap" Text="{Binding ChildName}" Style="{StaticResource
SubtitleTextStyle}"/>
    <TextBox TextWrapping="Wrap" Text="{Binding NewObservation.Text, Mode=TwoWay}"
Margin="0,10,10,0" Height="464"/>
</StackPanel>
```

Notice the binding on the TextBox, it's set to NewObservation.Text. Let's see what that's all about. Don't forget to change the DataContext for this page, it should be set to the same as the MainPage. We've got two properties on this page, as shown in Listing 4-9.

Listing 4-9. Properties

```
private Observation _newObservation;
public Observation NewObservation
{
    get { return _newObservation; }
    set
    {
        if (_newObservation == value) return;

        _newObservation = value;

        OnPropertyChanged("NewObservation");
    }
}

private string _childName;
public string ChildName
{
    get { return _childName; }
    set
    {
        if (_childName == value) return;

        _childName = value;

        OnPropertyChanged("ChildName");
    }
}
```

The first property is what the text box is bound too. It's an instance of the Observation class, and the property Text of that class is what's actually bound to the text box. The second property is just a text that's used to fill the text block. It is very important that you don't forget to set the binding mode to two-way binding on the text box or the entered values won't reflect back to the property.

AppBar

Next to the StackPanel, this ObservationPage also has an app bar, as shown in Listing 4-10.

Listing 4-10. AppBar

```
<common:LayoutAwarePage.BottomAppBar>
    <AppBar FontFamily="Global User Interface" Background="#E5746F6F">
        <StackPanel HorizontalAlignment="Left" Height="100" Width="1346" Orientation="Horizontal">
            <Button HorizontalAlignment="Stretch" VerticalAlignment="Stretch"
Style="{StaticResource SaveAppBarButtonStyle}" Click="Button_Click_1"/>
```

```
        </StackPanel>
    </AppBar>
</common:LayoutAwarePage.BottomAppBar>
```

The app bar has one button, so remember to uncomment the SaveAppBarButtonStyle in StandardStyles.xaml. The code behind the button is presented in Listing 4-11.

Listing 4-11. Save Button

```
private void Button_Click_1(object sender, RoutedEventArgs e)
{
    try
    {
        NewObservation.Date = DateTime.Today;
        App.Connection.InsertAsync(NewObservation);
        Frame.GoBack();
    }
    catch (Exception)
    {
        MessageDialog dialog = new MessageDialog("Something went wrong, please try again");

        dialog.ShowAsync();
    }
}
```

This is the code to add an item to the database. First, we set today's date to the Date property of NewObservation. We then call the InsertAsync function on the Connection property that we defined in App.xaml.cs. The InsertAsync function will look at the type of NewObservation, check if there's a table in the database that reflects that type, and finally insert the item into that table. To finish off, we navigate one step back on the navigation stack, putting us back on the MainPage.

Speaking of the MainPage, that one also has an app bar, as defined in the code in Listing 4-12.

Listing 4-12. AppBar XAML

```
<common:LayoutAwarePage.BottomAppBar>
    <AppBar FontFamily="Global User Interface" Background="#E5746F6F">
        <StackPanel HorizontalAlignment="Left" Height="100" Width="1346" Orientation="Horizontal">
            <Button HorizontalAlignment="Stretch" VerticalAlignment="Stretch"
Style="{StaticResource AddAppBarButtonStyle}" Click="Button_Click_1"/>
            <Button HorizontalAlignment="Stretch" VerticalAlignment="Stretch"
Style="{StaticResource CalendarDayAppBarButtonStyle}" Click="Button_Click_2"/>
        </StackPanel>
    </AppBar>
</common:LayoutAwarePage.BottomAppBar>
```

There are two buttons here: one to add a child to the database and a second one to view the history of all observations. Let's start with adding a child, first we navigate to the AddChildPage, using the code in Listing 4-13.

Listing 4-13. Navigation Button

```
private void Button_Click_1(object sender, RoutedEventArgs e)
{
    Frame.Navigate(typeof(AddChildPage));
}
```

Add Child Form

The logic behind adding a child is almost identical to that for adding an observation. Listing 4-14 provides the code for adding the child details.

Listing 4-14. Form for New Child

```
<StackPanel HorizontalAlignment="Left" Height="608" Margin="126,10,0,0" Grid.Row="1"
VerticalAlignment="Top" Width="976">
    <TextBlock TextWrapping="Wrap" Text="Firstname" Style="{StaticResource SubtitleTextStyle}"/>
    <TextBox TextWrapping="Wrap" Text="{Binding NewChild.Firstname, Mode=TwoWay}"
Margin="0,10,0,0"/>
    <TextBlock TextWrapping="Wrap" Text="Lastname" Style="{StaticResource SubtitleTextStyle}"
Margin="0,40,0,0"/>
    <TextBox TextWrapping="Wrap" Text="{Binding NewChild.Lastname, Mode=TwoWay}" Margin="0,10,0,0"/>
</StackPanel>
```

Figure 4-2 shows how the form will looks.

Figure 4-2. *The new child form*

Once again, there is an app bar on this page, and it is identical to the app bar on the ObservationPage, so copy it from there. The code to save a child is very similar as well, as provided in Listing 4-15.

Listing 4-15. Save Button

```
private async void Button_Click_1(object sender, RoutedEventArgs e)
{
    try
    {
        await App.Connection.InsertAsync(NewChild);

        NewChild = new Child();
    }
    catch (Exception)
    {
        MessageDialog dialog = new MessageDialog("Something went wrong, try again");
    }
}
```

Instead of navigating back to the previous page, we reinitialize the NewChild property, and this will clear the text boxes and allow us to rapidly add children without having to navigate back to this page every time.

Displaying Data on MainPage

We now have some children in our database and we can add observations for them. We want to load all the children when the app starts and display them on the MainPage. We do this with the code presented in Listing 4-16.

Listing 4-16. GetData Method

```
private async void GetData()
{
    try
    {
        Children = await App.Connection.Table<Child>().ToListAsync();
    }
    catch (Exception)
    {
        MessageDialog dialog = new MessageDialog("Something went wrong, try restarting the app");
    }
}
```

I would greatly advise calling this method from the OnNavigatedTo method because that method is surely executed. The constructor is only executed when the page is created. When you're using something like dependency injection, you'll always get the same existing instance of your MainPage whenever you navigate back to it. In that case, the constructor won't fire, but the OnNavigatedTo method will be hit, in our case effectively updating the data on the MainPage.

To load the children from the database we once again call upon the Connection property defined in App.xaml.cs. It has a Table<T> method where T is the type of the table that we want to retrieve. That result gets converted into a list, and that list is bound to the GridView on the MainPage.

Running the App

And with that this small app is finished. We can continue to add children and observations and can get a list of children and observations from the database and show them on the MainPage. SQLite has some other functionality like updating and deleting data, but calling those functions is identical to what we have done here so far. The problem with this app is that the data are really local. For example, let's say my wife buys a new device and installs the app there, none of the data on the old device will be available on the new device. In the next part, we'll take a look at using a REST service from within our Windows Store app. If you want to learn how to build REST services yourself, I would suggest you take a look at ASP.NET web API. It's really easy to get started with it, and if you already know ASP.NET MVC, you're off to a good start. The official ASP.NET web site (http://www.asp.net) has some great tutorials on getting started with ASP.NET web API.

Consuming REST Services

Using REST services is a very popular way of building an API. The way this works is that a certain URL is submitted containing the request from the user. The API gets the request from the URL, retrieves the data, optionally does some work with the data, serializes them in, for example, XML or JSON, and returns that serialized result to the requester, in our case the Windows Store app. It's then up to us to take that result and deserialize it into our Plain Old CLR Objects (POCOs).

REST services comprise client–server technology that works in a completely stateless way, meaning that no client information is stored on the server. Every client request contains all the information that the server needs. A RESTful web service is a service that is called using basic HTTP requests, and the header contains the data that the service needs while the URL can contain parameters for the service to respond with the correct data.

Twitter Search App

This section leads you through building a Twitter search application. To do read operations on the Twitter API, you don't need an API key. As soon as you want to log in or post tweets, you'll need to request one of those. CRUD operations of a REST service all look identical, but underneath they can be pretty diverse, depending on the technology that's being used. We'll only try for the read functionality, and that'll save us the hassle of requesting an API key.

The Tweet Class

As usual, we need to begin by creating a model, in this case a Tweet class, using the code in Listing 4-17.

Listing 4-17. Tweet Class

```
using Newtonsoft.Json;

namespace TwitterSearch.Model
{
    public class Tweet
    {
        [JsonProperty(PropertyName = "from_user_name")]
        public string User { get; set; }

        [JsonProperty(PropertyName = "text")]
        public string Message { get; set; }
    }
}
```

See the using statement? That includes a library called Json.net. The Twitter API returns JSON results, so we need to deserialize that into this Tweet class. The .NET has a built in serializer class, but Json.net is much faster and supports a lot more. If you are curious about the difference here, James Newton (the Json.net developer) has a nice comparison table and some speed graphs on his web site (http://james.newtonking.com/pages/json-net.aspx) that explain this. To add it, just search for Json.net on NuGet and click Install.

Now, about those two attributes. Properties in JSON tend to have some ugly looking names, such as from_user_name. As .NET developers, we usually don't like these. So give your property a useful name and give it the Jsonproperty(PropertyName) attribute, creating a form of mapping between the JSON property and the C# property. This will be the only model class we're going to use in this app.

MainPage

The next step is the MainPage. Here we'll have a text box, a button, and a GridView. Text entered into the text box will be sent to the Twitter API when the button is clicked. The code in Listing 4-18 will get you there.

Listing 4-18. MainPage XAML

```
<TextBox x:Name="QueryText" HorizontalAlignment="Left" Margin="125,10,0,0" Grid.Row="1"
TextWrapping="Wrap" VerticalAlignment="Top" Width="705" Height="32"/>
<Button Content="Search" HorizontalAlignment="Left" Margin="860,5,0,0" Grid.Row="1"
VerticalAlignment="Top" Height="38" Width="79" Click="Button_Click_1"/>
<GridView Grid.Row="2" Margin="125,0,0,0"
            ItemsSource="{Binding Tweets}">
    <GridView.ItemTemplate>
        <DataTemplate>
            <StackPanel>
                <TextBlock Text="{Binding User}" />
                <TextBlock Text="{Binding Message}" />
            </StackPanel>
        </DataTemplate>
    </GridView.ItemTemplate>
</GridView>
```

Once again, don't forget to set the correct DataContext to this page. The button click will call a method in our service class, and that service class will contact the Twitter API and interpret the results, as demonstrated with the code in Listing 4-19.

Listing 4-19. Button Click

```
private async void Button_Click_1(object sender, RoutedEventArgs e)
{
    TwitterService service = new TwitterService();

    Tweets = await service.GetTweets(QueryText.Text);
}
```

Then use the code in Listing 4-20 for the service itself.

Listing 4-20. Twitter Wrapper

```
public class TwitterService
{
    public async Task<List<Tweet>> GetTweets(string query)
    {
        var url = String.Format("http://search.twitter.com/search.json?q={0}", query);

        if (!NetworkInterface.GetIsNetworkAvailable())
        {
            MessageDialog dialog =
                new MessageDialog("No active internetconnection found, please connect to the
internet and try again");
            dialog.ShowAsync();

            return null;
        }
        else
        {
            HttpClient client = new HttpClient();

            var response = await client.GetAsync(url);
            string json = await response.Content.ReadAsStringAsync();

            JObject obj = JObject.Parse(json);
            var jsonResults = obj["results"];

            return await JsonConvert.DeserializeObjectAsync<List<Tweet>>(jsonResults.ToString());
        }

    }
}
```

Let's walk through this from top to bottom. First, the GetTweets function is marked as async. We don't know how long the Twitter service call will take to complete, so to prevent our user interface (UI) from freezing while we are waiting for the search result, we do this asynchronously. Next, we build the URL and pass in the query our user entered in the text box. The next line in the code is an important one to remember. This call will check if the device has an active network connection. This is pretty important since we're contacting an external service. Assuming we have a connection, we'll initialize an HttpClient and call its GetAsync method, passing in the URL as either a string or a uniform resource identifier (URI). What we will receive is an HttpResponseMessage. The next line will read the content in that response and we'll have our JSON string. Now the first part of that JSON is some diagnostic data, which we don't really need now. What we do need is the part named "results". To get that we first parse the JSON string into a JObject, and from there we can grab a part of the JSON, in this case the part called "results". Once we have that, we can deserialize it as a type of List<Tweet> and return that to the MainPage. The result should look like those shown in Figure 4-3.

Figure 4-3. *Search results from Twitter*

The `HttpClient` is the class that you'll need for all REST actions. Next to this Get method that we've just used, it can do Delete, Post, and Put or Insert and Update. And that works the same way as this Get method.

In the next and final section, we'll have a look at Windows Azure Mobile Services (WAMS).

Windows Azure Mobile Services

WAMS are basically Cloud-based services made easy. They are set up with a wizard in the Azure management portal. After the set up, you can download a solution from a Windows Store app that is already hooked up to the service. The only thing we need to do is create the UI and determine when to call the service. Let's start building one.

■ **Note** At the time of writing, WAMS is still in preview, and it might respond or look a bit different when it gets released. But the main functionality should remain the same.

Creating a Mobile Service

Let's get this thing created. We'll reuse the children observation data from the first part of this chapter, so we won't have to redo all the UI stuff. First, go to your Azure management portal and create a new Mobile Service, as shown in Figure 4-4.

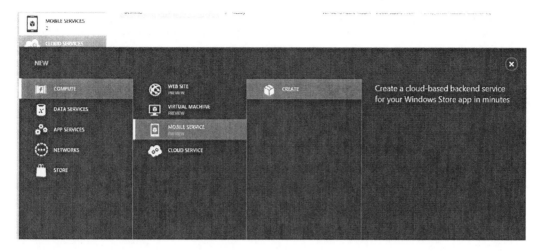

Figure 4-4. *The Azure portal*

Click Create to launch the setup wizard, as shown in Figure 4-5.

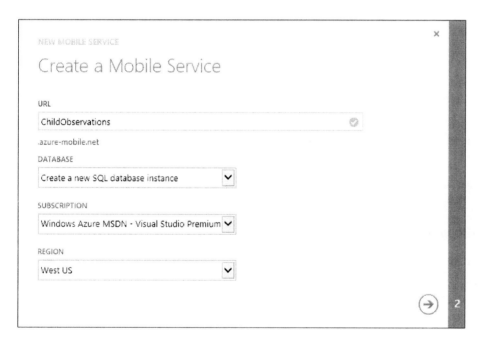

Figure 4-5. *Mobile Service wizard*

Fill in a URL, and it will check it. If it doesn't exist yet, it needs to be unique so the URL will be publically reachable. Also be sure to select Create a new SQL database instance. Then continue on to the next step, as shown in Figure 4-6.

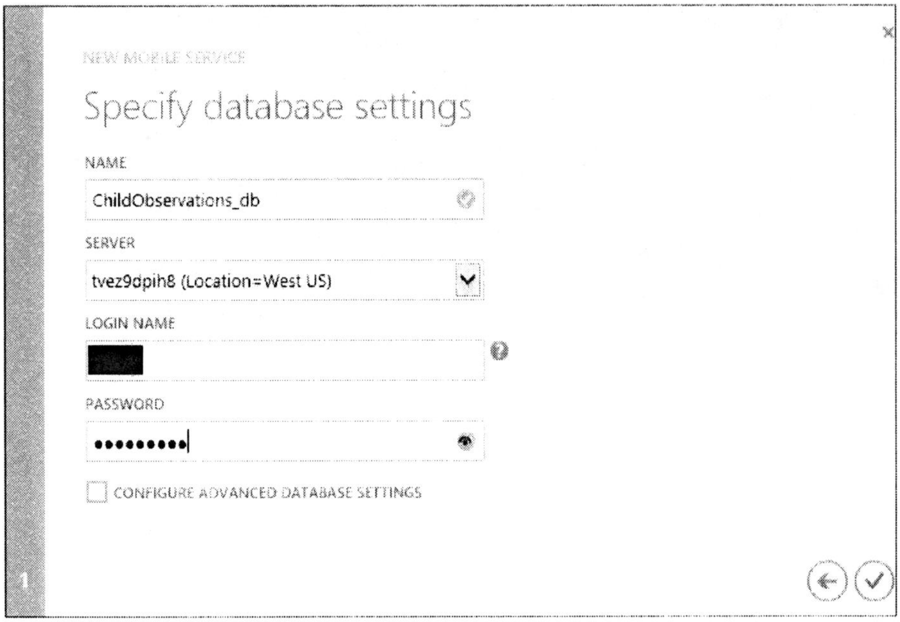

Figure 4-6. *Database settings for Mobile Service*

For the best performance, try to place the service and the database in the same data center, and the wizard will show a warning if you select different data centers for the service and database. Click OK and the notification in Figure 4-7 should show up.

≡ Creating the following mobile service: 'ChildObservations'

Figure 4-7. *Mobile Service being created*

When the creation is finished, open up the details and you will be greeted by the page shown in Figure 4-8.

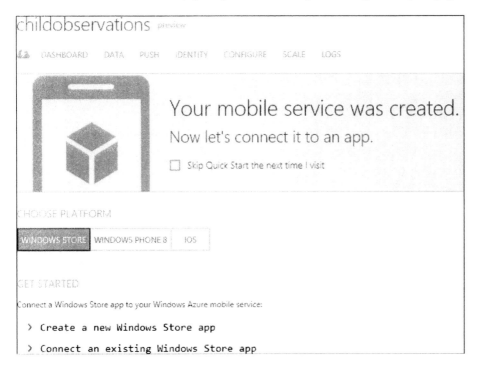

Figure 4-8. Mobile Service created

At this time, WAMS is available for Windows 8, Windows Phone 8, and iOS. It should be available for Windows Phone 7 and Android soon. Choose Windows Store and click Create a new Windows Store app. The page will slide open and allow you to download the WAMS SDK, as shown in Figure 4-9.

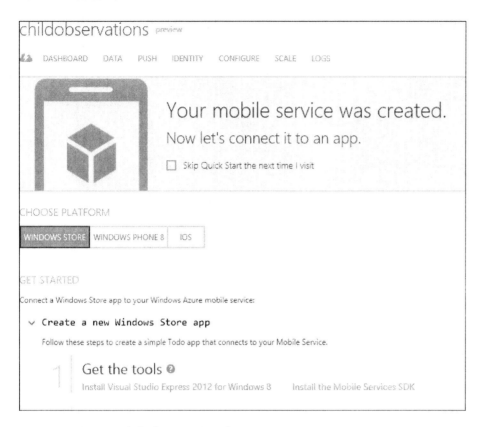

Figure 4-9. Supported platforms at time of writing

The SDK itself is really small, it took me under two minutes to download and install it. This page also allows you to create a test table in the database, but we won't be doing that. We'll immediately create our real database. On top of the page, select Data ➤ Add a table, as shown in Figure 4-10.

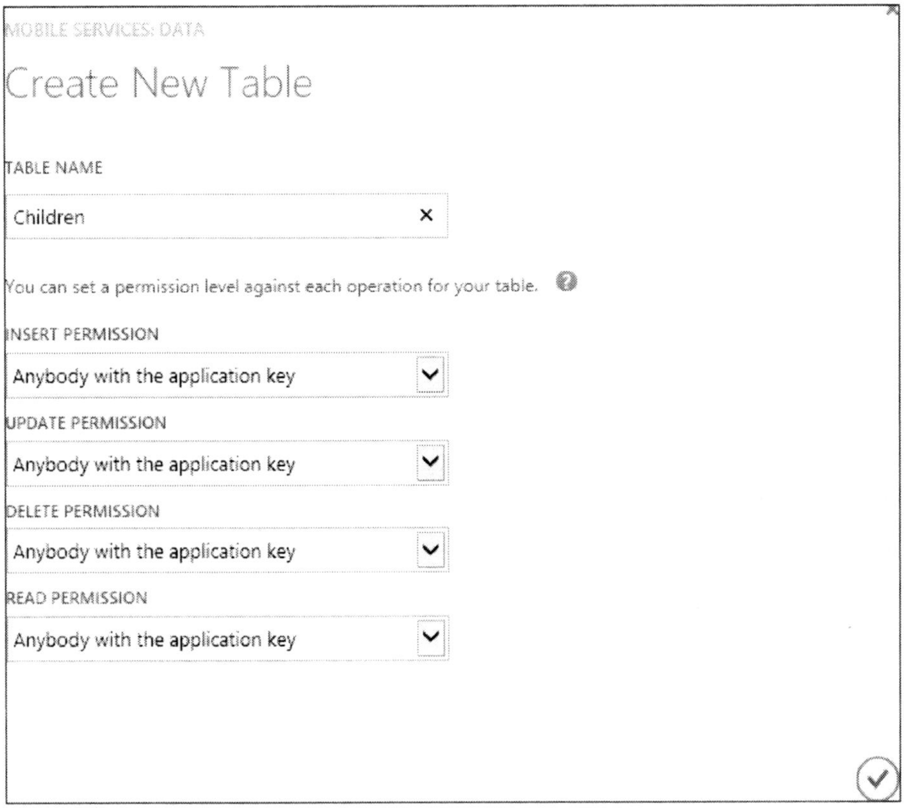

Figure 4-10. *Permissions for Mobile Service*

Give the table a name. This is also the place to set permissions for every CRUD operation on this table. Figure 4-11 shows the different options.

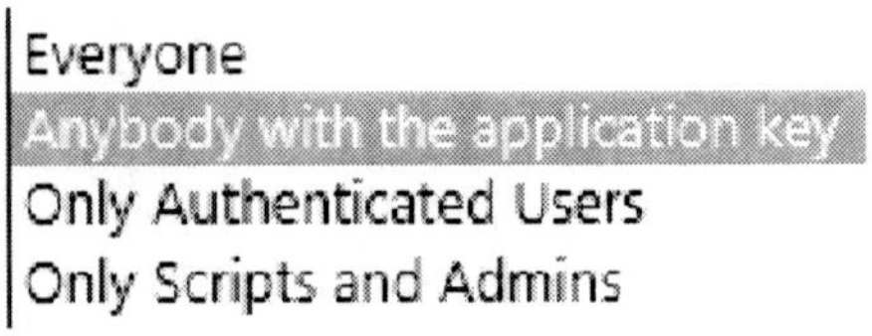

Figure 4-11. *Permission options*

The first three options allow changes from within the app, the fourth one only allows changes from within the Azure management.

Creating the Windows Store App

All right, time to create the app itself. For now, we'll just allow the possibility to create children, but feel free to expand the app to also create observations. It will be a great exercise.

Download the solution from Azure Mobile Services and open it. You'll see that it is hooked up to our service but it doesn't use the Children table that we've just created. Instead it's a demo app for a list of to-do items. Start by creating the Children class just as we did earlier in the SQLite part of this chapter. Use the code in Listing 4-21.

Listing 4-21. Children Class

```
public class Children
{
    public int Id { get; set; }
    public string Firstname { get; set; }
    public string Lastname { get; set; }
}
```

Now let's clean up the MainPage code a bit, using the code provided in Listing 4-22.

Listing 4-22. MainPage Class

```
public sealed partial class MainPage : Page, INotifyPropertyChanged
{
    private List<Children> _childrenList;
    public List<Children> Children
    {
        get { return _childrenList; }
        set
        {
            if (_childrenList == value) return;

            _childrenList = value;

            OnPropertyChanged("Children");
        }
    }

    // MobileServiceCollectionView implements ICollectionView (useful for databinding to lists) and
    // is integrated with your Mobile Service to make it easy to bind your data to the ListView
    private IMobileServiceTable<Children> _childrenTable = App.MobileService.GetTable<Children>();

    public MainPage()
    {
        this.InitializeComponent();
    }

    private void LoadAllChildren()
    {
        // This code refreshes the entries in the list view be querying the TodoItems table.
        // The query excludes completed TodoItems
        Children = await _childrenTable.ToListAsync();
    }
```

```
protected override void OnNavigatedTo(NavigationEventArgs e)
{
    LoadAllChildren();
}

private void Button_Click_1(object sender, RoutedEventArgs e)
{
    Frame.Navigate(typeof (AddChildPage));
}

public event PropertyChangedEventHandler PropertyChanged;

private void OnPropertyChanged(string propertyName = null)
{
    PropertyChangedEventHandler handler = PropertyChanged;
    if (handler != null) handler(this, new PropertyChangedEventArgs(propertyName));
}
}
```

The MobileServiceCollectionView can be bound to controls accepting ItemsSource and so on.
IMobileServiceTable<T> is what we use to reference tables in the SQL Azure database. The
App.MobileService.GetTable<T> method does not return any data from the table. It just sets the reference to the
table. We need to explicitly execute a command like ToCollectionView() to get data from the database in our view.

We of course need to input data before we can retrieve it, so copy over the AddChildPage from the other project
but instead of inserting a new child into a SQLite database, save it as shown in Listing 4-23.

Listing 4-23. NewChild Property

```
private Children _newChild;
public Children NewChild
{
    get { return _newChild; }
    set
    {
        if (_newChild == value) return;

        _newChild = value;

        OnPropertyChanged("NewChild");
    }
}

private IMobileServiceTable<Children> _childrenTable = App.MobileService.GetTable<Children>();

private async void Button_SaveChild(object sender, RoutedEventArgs e)
{
    try
    {
        await _childrenTable.InsertAsync(NewChild);
```

```
        NewChild = new Children();
    }
    catch (Exception)
    {
        MessageDialog dialog = new MessageDialog("Something went wrong, try again");
    }
}
```

We need the same reference to the table as seen on the MainPage. Once we have that, we can just call InsertAsync() on that table to insert a child. Go ahead and try it.

It worked? Great. But wait, we did create a table on our database, but we never defined any columns, so how did our child get saved correctly? Check out the Configure tab on your Mobile Service in the Azure management portal. Do you see the Dynamic schema setting? That allows the generation of columns whenever an item is inserted with a property that doesn't have a column yet (Figure 4-12). This is a really awesome feature, but remember to switch it off once your app is launched.

childobservations preview

DASHBOARD   DATA   PUSH   IDENTITY   CONFIGURE   SCALE   LOGS

database settings

SQL DATABASE   ChildObservations_db (server: tvez9dpih8)

dynamic schema

ENABLE DYNAMIC SCHEMA   ON   OFF

Figure 4-12. Dynamic schema setting

Summary

There are a variety of ways of storing data from an application. The least expensive way is to use SQLite databases, which are stored locally on the device. The biggest disadvantage here is that the data from the user are not available on all the user's devices. On the other hand, there are REST services. REST services are widely used for public API services and are easy to implement. The disadvantage here is that you need to develop them and create your database, so you lose quite a bit of time, but you win a lot of flexibility and reliability.

This is where Windows Azure Mobile Services comes in. WAMS provides a quick, wizard-driven way to create a service. Once that's done, you just create your classes in your app, and as soon as the app contacts the service, all the columns are "automagically" generated for you. WAMS is a really easy to use, very lightweight SDK, and spending less time on your service means you can spend more time on the app itself. If your API needs to contain a lot of business logic, it can get a bit more difficult to use WAMS. WAMS is built on top of node.js, and you can expand the basic scripts using the Azure portal. It might be more interesting to build a REST service when you need a logic-heavy service, but that's really up to you to decide.

In the next chapter, we'll have a look at those shiny buttons on the right side of your screen called the charms. We'll have a look at how to implement them in our apps so that the apps feel like they are really a part of the operating system.

CHAPTER 5

Build a Charming Application

With Windows 8, Microsoft introduced the concept of charms. *Charms* provide a uniform way to do tasks that are found throughout the majority of applications, such as searching and settings. In this era of sharing all possible sorts of content on a wide variety of social networks, Microsoft decided to throw in a Share charm as well. The charms can be found by placing the mouse in the upper right corner of the screen or on a touch-enabled device by dragging in from the right edge of the screen.

The so-called Charms bar contains five buttons, as shown in Figure 5-1. The middle one is actually not really a charm, it's more a Start button, navigating the user back to the Start screen when clicked. The most interesting ones for us are Search, Share, and Settings. We can leverage the power behind those charms in our own apps, and this chapter will go over them one by one. We'll start at the top of the charms bar and work our way to the bottom.

Figure 5-1. The five charms

We'll be implementing the use of the charms in a booking application for hotels. The MainPage shows an overview of a bunch of hotels. Users can select a hotel to view the details. The charms will be used to search for a hotel, to share a hotel experience with friends, and to adjust the app's settings. I'm ready to go, if you're ready as well, we can start implementing those charms.

Search Charm

First up is the Search charm, which allows us to search inside our applications. A good example of this is the Store app that is installed by default in Windows 8. The cool thing about this Search function is that the app itself does not need to be started first. When the Search charm is clicked, it will show a list of all search-enabled apps installed on the system. When one is clicked, the app will open and navigate immediately to the search results page, as shown in Figure 5-2, effectively saving us a few clicks.

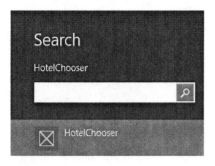

Figure 5-2. *Search charm*

The Search charm is one of the easiest of all charms to implement. Basically, all you need to do is add a `SearchResultPage` to your project, provide the search logic in its code behind, and you're good to go. Right-click your project then Add ➤ Add New Item. Select Search Contract from the dialog box, as shown in the screenshot in Figure 5-3, give it any name you want (but choose wisely), and click Add. Visual Studio now adds the page to your solution and overrides the `OnSearchActivated` method, as in Listing 5-1.

Listing 5-1. OnSearchActivated Method

```
protected override void OnSearchActivated(Windows.ApplicationModel.Activation.
SearchActivatedEventArgs args)
{
    ComicDB.View.SearchResultsPage.Activate(args.QueryText, args.PreviousExecutionState);
}
```

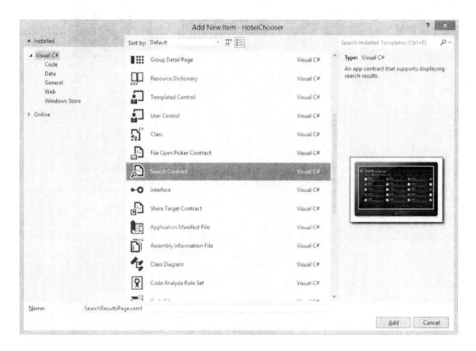

Figure 5-3. *Adding the Search contract*

The page itself is a LayoutAwarePage with a title, Back button, and ItemsControl, GridView, and ListView. The ListView is used for the snapped view and the GridView is what will contain the search results when in full screen mode. We'll take a closer look at the ItemsControl a bit later, for now it suffices to know that it's used to display the available filters and the number of results for that filter. When the app is snapped, the filters will be shown in a combo box with the results as a ListView. All this is part of the Search Contract template, so we get it for free. We do, however, need to implement the search logic ourselves, obviously.

Let's take a look at the code behind the Search page. Already there is quite a lot of stuff there, such as variables for the query text, selection changed event handlers to deal with the filters, the load state event handler, and so on. Microsoft provides us with a very clear indication of the lines we need to complete in the code to get the search to actually return results. Let's scroll down to the LoadState method, which looks like the code in Listing 5-2.

Listing 5-2. LoadState Method

```
protected override void LoadState(Object navigationParameter, Dictionary<String, Object> pageState)
    {
        var queryText = navigationParameter as String;
        // TODO: Application-specific searching logic.  The search process is responsible for
        // creating a list of user-selectable result categories:
        //
        // filterList.Add(new Filter("<filter name>", <result count>));
        // Only the first filter, typically "All", should pass true as a third argument in
        //order to start in an active state.  Results for the active filter are provided
        // in Filter_SelectionChanged below.

        var filterList = new List<Filter>();
        filterList.Add(new Filter("All", 0, true));

        // Communicate results through the view model
        this.DefaultViewModel["QueryText"] = '\u201c' + queryText +  '\u201d';
        this.DefaultViewModel["Filters"] = filterList;
        this.DefaultViewModel["ShowFilters"] = filterList.Count > 1;
    }
```

This method is called when the page gets instantiated. The block of comments is where we need to set our search logic. We get a variable containing the search query entered by the user. It's now up to us to get the collection of items that contains this query. In our case, we'll allow users to search for the name of a hotel. We could later expand the functionality by allowing users to search for hotels with a certain amount of stars. Replace the TODO comment with this line of code:

```
var searchResults = DataStore.GetAllHotels().Where(h =>
h.Name.ToLower().Contains(queryText.ToLower())).ToList();
```

DataStore is the class that we use to get our data. In a real-life project, we could use that class to access our service or database, but in this sample it just returns a collection of hard-coded objects. The GetAllHotels method should speak for itself. To filter the needed results out, we'll use a Lambda statement. Just to be safe, the code first converts all hotel names and the query text to lower case characters just to make it case insensitive. Then we just filter out every hotel with a name that contains the queryText. Be sure to use .Contains() here instead of checking if it's equal or the user will need to enter the exact name of the hotel to get any results.

We've got a list of results, so now we need to pass it through to some bindable object so our page can actually show the results. Since the SearchResultPage template inherits from the LayoutAwarePage, we have a DefaultViewModel property at our disposal. This property is of type IObservableMap, the MSDN documentation on this type says:

Notifies event handlers of dynamic changes to a map, such as when items get added or removed.

Basically, we have something like an observable dictionary here that we can bind to in our XAML code. The default XAML binding in the template expects a key called "Results" with the list of found results as its value. Let's complete this example by adding the key/value pair to the property. In the code, right after our search logic, add this piece of code:

```
DefaultViewModel["Results"] = searchResults;
```

The completed LoadState event handler looks like the code presented in Listing 5-3.

Listing 5-3. LoadState with Search Logic

```
protected override void LoadState(Object navigationParameter, Dictionary<String, Object> pageState)
        {
            var queryText = navigationParameter as String;

            var searchResults = DataStore.GetAllHotels().Where(h =>
h.Name.ToLower().Contains(queryText.ToLower())).ToList();

                var filterList = new List<Filter>();
                filterList.Add(new Filter("All", 0, true));

                // Communicate results through the view model
                DefaultViewModel["QueryText"] = '\u201c' + queryText + '\u201d';
                DefaultViewModel["Filters"] = filterList;
                DefaultViewModel["ShowFilters"] = filterList.Count > 1;
        }
```

With this, everything is in order to get our first search results! I mentioned in the beginning of this chapter that we can just launch the Search charm and start searching. Although this is true for apps installed from the store, we do need to launch an app that is under development first. That's because running an app for the first time also installs it on your system, and an app needs to be installed on your system to be able to leverage the charms. I would suggest that when developing the charms you launch the app every time you want to test charm capabilities, and that will ensure that your latest changes are in the version installed on your system. Be sure to test the Search charm from outside the app once the feature is completed, and definitely try to launch the app from the Search charm and press the Back button to see what happens—things tend to go wrong there. Figure 5-4 shows the results of launching our search app.

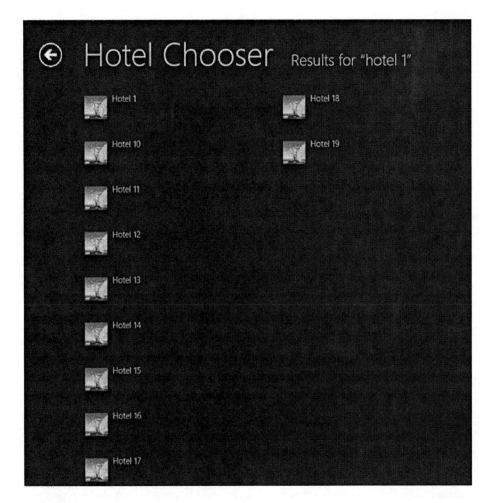

Figure 5-4. *Search results in the app*

Filters

Now that we've got our searching charm implemented, it's time to offer some filtering to our users. Filtering provides an easy way for the users of your app to work through the search results to find the result they actually need. In our example of the hotel chooser app, we'll provide a filter for each separate country in the search results.

All that's needed for filters to do their magic is already included in the SearchPage template. Scroll down a bit from the LoadState method to find the code provided in Listing 5-4.

Listing 5-4. *Filter Selection*

```
void Filter_SelectionChanged(object sender, SelectionChangedEventArgs e)
    {
        // Determine what filter was selected
        var selectedFilter = e.AddedItems.FirstOrDefault() as Filter;
```

```
                    if (selectedFilter != null)
                    {
                        // Mirror the results into the corresponding Filter object to allow the
                        // RadioButton representation used when not snapped to reflect the change
                        selectedFilter.Active = true;

                        // TODO: Respond to the change in active filter by setting
this.DefaultViewModel["Results"]
                        //          to a collection of items with bindable Image, Title, Subtitle, and
Description properties

                        // Ensure results are found
                        object results;
                        ICollection resultsCollection;
                        if (this.DefaultViewModel.TryGetValue("Results", out results) &&
                            (resultsCollection = results as ICollection) != null &&
                            resultsCollection.Count != 0)
                        {
                            VisualStateManager.GoToState(this, "ResultsFound", true);
                            return;
                        }
                    }

                    // Display informational text when there are no search results.
                    VisualStateManager.GoToState(this, "NoResultsFound", true);
                }
```

Again, we find a TODO comment. The method determines what filter is selected, checks if the filter actually contains items, and switches the VisualState to either show the results or show a message stating that no items have been found. What we need to do is filter the results based on the selected filter and pass those filtered results into the ViewModel. That means we'll need the results in the Filter_SelectionChanged method. We can either do a new call to our data store when the filter changed, or, because our first filter contains all the results, we can reuse that collection for lightning fast performance. That works in our case, but in bigger apps it is best to contact the service again and execute a new query. The data might have changed after all. To start off, create a class-wide private variable that will contain the results, as shown in Listing 5-5.

Listing 5-5. SearchResultsPage

```
public sealed partial class SearchResultsPage : HotelChooser.Common.LayoutAwarePage
    {
        private List<Hotel> _searchResults;

        public SearchResultsPage()
        {
            this.InitializeComponent();
        }
```

I've put the constructor and class declaration here as well just to give you an idea where to put the variable. Next, in the LoadState method, replace this line:

```
var searchResults = DataStore.GetAllHotels().Where(h =>
h.Name.ToLower().Contains(queryText.ToLower())).ToList();
```

with this line:

```
_searchResults = DataStore.GetAllHotels().Where(h =>
h.Name.ToLower().Contains(queryText.ToLower())).ToList();
```

This puts the search results in the class-wide variable instead of the one created inside the LoadState method. Now that we can reach our results throughout the SearchPage class, we can start filtering them. First, we'll add the filter. Filters are set up much like the way the results are bound to the view, by using the ViewModel. In the case of the filters, we're using a key named Filters by default. The value is a list of type Filter, which should already be created inside the LoadState method. It's part of the page template. The page displays the filter names with the number of results next to them. In order to do this, it's up to us to pass the amount of results into the Filter object, and the Filter class is defined beneath the SearchResultsPage class. By default there's only one filter defined, which is named "All", and 0 is passed in as the amount. Let's start off by fixing that in this line:

```
filterList.Add(new Filter("All", 0, true));
```

Replace the 0 with _searchResults.Count so it looks like this:

```
filterList.Add(new Filter("All", _searchResults.Count, true));
```

And that's it, the "All" filter now gets the correct result count passed in. Easy, right? The next step is to add our filter. Since I live in Belgium, we'll start off with that. Under the line that adds the "All" filter, add this line of code:

```
filterList.Add(new Filter("Belgium", _searchResults.Count(r => r.Country.ToLower() == "belgium"),
false));
```

And just like that we've added a new filter. The next step is to change the results view whenever the user changes the filter. This is done in the Filter_SelectionChanged event handler, as mentioned a few lines back. Change the TODO comment with the code block given in Listing 5-6.

Listing 5-6. Filter Handling

```
switch (selectedFilter.Name.ToLower())
{
    case "all":
        DefaultViewModel["Results"] = _searchResults;
        break;
    case "belgium":
        DefaultViewModel["Results"] = _searchResults.Where(r => r.Country.ToLower() ==
"belgium").ToList();
        break;
}
```

Here we're checking the selectedFilter name, but first we're converting it to lower case just to be safe. Then, in the case that the user selected Belgium as the filter, we're passing in the results that have Belgium as a country. Now when we fire up the app and search for "hotel 1" we get the result shown in Figure 5-5.

Figure 5-5. *Search filters*

Go ahead and switch back and forth between the two filters, they should react instantaneously.

Having fun so far? I know I am. Let's take the Search charm a bit further. Let me start off by showing you what we'll be doing next. I assume you're currently working on a Windows 8–powered machine. Open the Store app so that you're on the main screen of the app. Now just start typing, you'll notice that by starting to type, the Search pane will pop open and you're filling in a search query. This is a very cool feature if your app relies on searching. Implementing it is almost as easy as using it. Let's take a look at how to do this.

We're going to enable this feature from the MainPage's constructor so that it gets enabled when the app is launched. The constructor's code currently looks like that provided in Listing 5-7.

Listing 5-7. MainPage Constructor

```
public MainPage()
{
    InitializeComponent();
    LoadData();
}
```

Let's adjust it so it looks like the code in Listing 5-8.

Listing 5-8. Modified Constructor

```
public MainPage()
{
    InitializeComponent();
    var searchPane = SearchPane.GetForCurrentView();
    searchPane.ShowOnKeyboardInput = true;

    LoadData();
}
```

Let me explain what happens here. The charms all launch a so-called pane, a flyout containing the UI for that charm. In the case of the Search charm, the pane is the part where you enter a query and can select any app containing a search contract. SearchPane is a sealed class in the Windows RT framework, providing all the events and logic for the Search charm. By calling the static method GetForCurrentView(), we can set a variable to the instance of the SearchPane for our current app. Once we have that, we can start setting properties or adding event handlers and so on. What we need to do here is set the ShowOnKeyboardInput property to true, however, be aware that this will pick up every keyboard input, even if a text box has focus, so be careful with this. That's all we need to do in order for the Search pane to show up when we start typing from inside the app. By the way, this also works from the Windows 8 Start screen to search for any app installed on the system.

Search Suggestions from a List

Now that we've got a pretty great search system, it's time to provide our users with suggestions for that search. Windows 8 provides a variety of ways to show suggestions, both from local and from remote sources.

The suggestions appear under the search text box, and the list is limited to a maximum of five suggestions. Let's start with providing suggestions from a list that's defined inside the app. The biggest advantage of this is that the results appear blazing fast since they're loaded into the memory on app start. The list itself is nothing special. It's just an array of countries that I borrowed from MSDN. The next step is to handle the SuggestionsRequested event from the SearchPane class. These steps are usually done in the App.xaml.cs file in the OnLaunched or OnActivated event. Let's walk through the steps.

First, we create two variables in the App.xaml.cs: the first will contain the SearchPane instance, the second is the list of search suggestions. The code in Listing 5-9 will get us there.

Listing 5-9. *Fields*

```
private SearchPane _searchPane;
private static readonly string[] SuggestionList =
    {
        "Shanghai", "Istanbul", "Karachi", "Delhi", "Mumbai", "Moscow", "São Paulo", "Seoul",
"Beijing", "Jakarta",
        "Tokyo", "Mexico City", "Kinshasa", "New York City", "Lagos", "London", "Lima", "Bogota",
"Tehran", "Ho Chi Minh City",
        "Hong Kong", "Bangkok", "Dhaka", "Cairo", "Hanoi", "Rio de Janeiro", "Lahore", "Chonquing",
"Bengaluru", "Tianjin",
        "Baghdad", "Riyadh", "Singapore", "Santiago", "Saint Petersburg", "Surat", "Chennai",
"Kolkata", "Yangon", "Guangzhou",
        "Alexandria", "Shenyang", "Hyderabad", "Ahmedabad", "Ankara", "Johannesburg", "Wuhan", "Los
Angeles", "Yokohama",
        "Abidjan", "Busan", "Cape Town", "Durban", "Pune", "Jeddah", "Berlin", "Pyongyang",
"Kanpur", "Madrid", "Jaipur",
        "Nairobi", "Chicago", "Houston", "Philadelphia", "Phoenix", "San Antonio", "San Diego",
"Dallas", "San Jose",
        "Jacksonville", "Indianapolis", "San Francisco", "Austin", "Columbus", "Fort Worth",
"Charlotte", "Detroit",
        "El Paso", "Memphis", "Baltimore", "Boston", "Seattle Washington", "Nashville", "Denver",
"Louisville", "Milwaukee",
        "Portland", "Las Vegas", "Oklahoma City", "Albuquerque", "Tucson", "Fresno", "Sacramento",
"Long Beach", "Kansas City",
        "Mesa", "Virginia Beach", "Atlanta", "Colorado Springs", "Omaha", "Raleigh", "Miami",
"Cleveland", "Tulsa", "Oakland",
```

```
        "Minneapolis", "Wichita", "Arlington", " Bakersfield", "New Orleans", "Honolulu", "Anaheim",
"Tampa", "Aurora",
        "Santa Ana", "St. Louis", "Pittsburgh", "Corpus Christi", "Riverside", "Cincinnati",
"Lexington", "Anchorage",
        "Stockton", "Toledo", "St. Paul", "Newark", "Greensboro", "Buffalo", "Plano", "Lincoln",
"Henderson", "Fort Wayne",
        "Jersey City", "St. Petersburg", "Chula Vista", "Norfolk", "Orlando", "Chandler", "Laredo",
"Madison", "Winston-Salem",
        "Lubbock", "Baton Rouge", "Durham", "Garland", "Glendale", "Reno", "Hialeah", "Chesapeake",
"Scottsdale",
        "North Las Vegas", "Irving", "Fremont", "Irvine", "Birmingham", "Rochester", "San
Bernardino", "Spokane",
        "Toronto", "Montreal", "Vancouver", "Ottawa-Gatineau", "Calgary", "Edmonton", "Quebec City",
"Winnipeg", "Hamilton"
    };
```

Now for all the magic! For this example I've used the OnLaunched event, but as mentioned before, it's also perfectly safe to use the OnActivated event. In the OnLaunched event, we first need to get the SearchPane instance and register an event handler for the SuggestionsRequested event, using this code:

```
_searchPane = SearchPane.GetForCurrentView();
_searchPane.SuggestionsRequested += OnSuggestionsRequested;
```

And finally, the OnSuggestionsRequested method, using the code in Listing 5-10.

Listing 5-10. OnSuggestionsRequested Method

```
private void OnSuggestionsRequested(SearchPane sender, SearchPaneSuggestionsRequestedEventArgs args)
{
    var queryText = args.QueryText;

    var request = args.Request;
    foreach (string suggestion in SuggestionList)
    {
        if (suggestion.StartsWith(queryText, StringComparison.CurrentCultureIgnoreCase))
        {
            //Add suggestion to Search Pane
            request.SearchSuggestionCollection.AppendQuerySuggestion(suggestion);

            //Search Pane can show at most 5 suggestions
            if (request.SearchSuggestionCollection.Size >= 5)
            {
                break;
            }
        }
    }
}
```

The class SearchPaneSuggestionsRequestedEventArgs contains the query that the user is currently entering. The SuggestionsRequested event will fire on every keystroke from the user. The code will cycle through all suggestions in the full list, checks if it contains the query entered by the user, and if it does, it passes the suggestion to the SearchPane. After five found results, the loop breaks off. The results look like those shown in Figure 5-6.

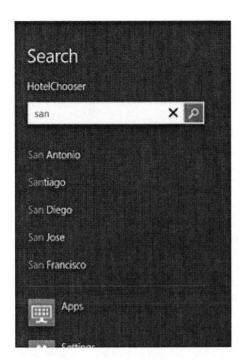

Figure 5-6. *Search suggestions*

Search Suggestions from Known Folders

Another way of providing suggestions is by suggesting the files inside one of the so-called known folders. The known folders live in the Windows.Storage namespace and are a list of constants, each pointing to a folder that exists on every Windows installation, folders such as My Documents and Pictures. The complete list available from Visual Studio is shown in Figure 5-7.

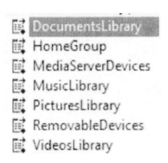

Figure 5-7. *Known folders*

Our hotel app doesn't really have a need for a suggestion list based on files inside one of those known folders, but for this argument's sake, we'll implement it anyway. Just like with the hard-coded list, we need to set this up in App.xaml.cs in an OnLaunched or an OnActivated event. Unlike the previous setup, we do not need to implement our own event handler to fill up the list. We just need to specify the folder and the file type that we're searching for, as in the code in Listing 5-11.

Listing 5-11. Getting the SearchPane

```
var settings = new LocalContentSuggestionSettings();
settings.Enabled = true;

if (settings.Enabled)
{
    settings.Locations.Add(KnownFolders.PicturesLibrary);
    settings.AqsFilter = "kind:pics";
}

SearchPane.GetForCurrentView().SetLocalContentSuggestionSettings(settings);
```

First, we need a variable of type LocalContentSuggestionSettings. This class does exactly as its name implies—it has settings for the suggestions. The first step is to enable the settings so we can use them. Then we add one or more locations to the Locations list. The Locations property is an IList of type StorageFolder, thus it can contain as many folders as you would like. The next property is a bit special. AqsFilter is a string that will specify what file types are being shown in the suggestion list. Advanced Query Syntax (AQS) is used by Windows Search, among others, and can be used in our app to specify the file type, author, or other file properties. If you want to read more about AQS, MSDN has a complete table with all possible filters and properties (http://msdn.microsoft.com/en-us/library/aa965711(v=VS.85).aspx).

There is one important step that's easy to overlook but essential to get search suggestions from your files. In your solution, double-click the Package.appxmanifest file and browse to the Capabilities tab, as shown in Figure 5-8. Every known folder has a check box there. We need to check the box for every folder that we need to access from within our app. However, this is only needed when we're accessing the folder from code. The user can freely browse the folder from a FilePicker, for example, without us setting the capability. If we should forget this step, we would get an access-denied error. Feel free to try running the app and using the Search charm without checking the check box.

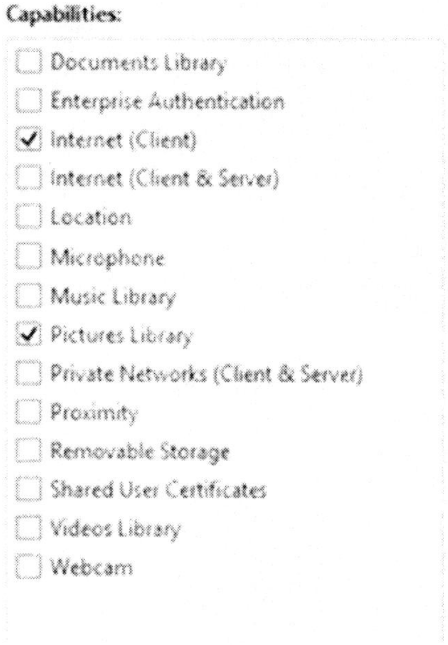

Capabilities:

- ☐ Documents Library
- ☐ Enterprise Authentication
- ☑ Internet (Client)
- ☐ Internet (Client & Server)
- ☐ Location
- ☐ Microphone
- ☐ Music Library
- ☑ Pictures Library
- ☐ Private Networks (Client & Server)
- ☐ Proximity
- ☐ Removable Storage
- ☐ Shared User Certificates
- ☐ Videos Library
- ☐ Webcam

Figure 5-8. *App capabilities*

That's actually all there is to it. When you start the app end search for something, as shown in Figure 5-9, it should suggest names of images inside the Pictures folder of Windows.

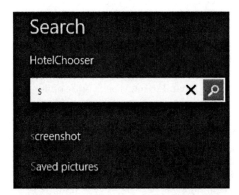

Figure 5-9. Suggestions from folders

Search Suggestions Through Open Search

The app is looking pretty cool so far, right? Now enough of all those local suggestions, we're living in an always connected world after all. Let's get some suggestions from an online source. One way to do this is to make use of the Open Search. Open Search is a collection of technologies that allows search results to be published in a syndicate form, allowing it to be aggregated. Open Search was developed by A9, a subsidiary of Amazon.

Basically, Open Search is a standard that is pretty widely used. If you're using an external API of some sorts and it supports Open Search, then it can provide suggestions for our app. Let's adjust our hotel app again and provide some search suggestions from Wikipedia.

First things first. To get the suggestions, we need to search, and find, the URL for the Open Search service. For Wikipedia that is http://en.wikipedia.org/w/api.php?action=opensearch&search={searchTerms}. This is the notation that needs to be used inside a Windows Store app to leverage the Open Search functionality.

The first thing we need to do is once again build an event handler for the SuggestionsRequested event, just as we did with the hard-coded list. In the event handler, we once again receive the query, but this time we need to send it over the wire to the Open Search service. Doing all this will probably take more than 50 milliseconds, meaning we'll need to do this asynchronously. Listing 5-12 shows what the signature of the function that will retrieve the data from the service looks like.

Listing 5-12. GetSuggestionsAsync Method Signature

```
private async Task GetSuggestionsAsync(string url, SearchSuggestionCollection suggestions)
{
...
}
```

Notice the async mark? The async keyword is new in .NET 4.5 and Windows RT. When a method is marked as async, it will run on the current synchronization thread when executed with the await keyword. An async method can only have Void, Task, or Task<T> as a return type. Void is actually only there to support async event handlers. Your own methods should return a Task where possible. To call async methods, you could use two methods. The first is plain and simple fire and forget. You call it as you would call any other method. The second one is the interesting one, you call the method by using the await keyword like this:

```
await GetSuggestionsAsync(@"http://www.example.com", request.SearchSuggestionCollection);
```

What will happen here is that the GetSuggestionsAsync method will start running on a separate thread, but instead of defining an OnEventCompleted callback, the method where the async function was called will halt its operations until the async method has finished. Once it's finished, the caller will resume his or her own actions. Effectively using async/await will ensure that your app is fast, fluid, and responsive. The compiler will take this very simplistic code and turn it into the spaghetti we used to know as threads, callbacks, and so on. When you're building an app that you plan to put on the Windows Store, be sure to use await/async every time an instruction might take more than 50 milliseconds or your app will fail certification.

Back to our app we go. The next thing we need is a *deferral*, an object that allows the app to retrieve the search suggestions asynchronously. After we get all of those, we need some error handling in case the suggestion search is cancelled, for example, when the user typed in another character. We want the current search to cancel, and we launch a new one whenever that happens. We're doing it that way because of the latency that might occur when targeting an online service. If we were to wait for every async call, then we would never get search suggestions in time. We also need to catch any errors from occurring or we would lose the suggestions altogether. And last, when everything has completed, we need to call the deferral's Complete event to finish up. First, we need to declare some extra variables in the App.xaml.cs class using this code:

```
private Task<string> _currentHttpTask;
private HttpClient _httpClient;
```

Listing 5-13 provides the code for the event handler.

Listing 5-13. Event Handler

```
private async void OnSuggestionsRequestedOpenSearch(SearchPane sender,
SearchPaneSuggestionsRequestedEventArgs args)
{
    var queryText = args.QueryText;
    string url = @"http://en.wikipedia.org/w/api.php?action=opensearch&search={searchTerms}";

    // The deferral object is used to supply suggestions asynchronously for example when fetching
suggestions from a web service.
    var request = args.Request;
    var deferral = request.GetDeferral();

    try
    {
        await GetSuggestionsAsync(Regex.Replace(url, "{searchTerms}",
Uri.EscapeDataString(queryText)), request.SearchSuggestionCollection);
    }
    catch (TaskCanceledException)
    {
        // task cancelled
    }
    catch (Exception)
    {
        //catch all other exceptions
        //you might want to do something useful here
```

```
    }
    finally
    {
        deferral.Complete();
    }
}
```

And then we add the code for the asynchronous method that will get the suggestions from the service, as provided in Listing 5-14.

Listing 5-14. GetSuggestionsAsync Method

```
private async Task GetSuggestionsAsync(string url, SearchSuggestionCollection suggestions)
{
    // Cancel the previous suggestion request if it is not finished.
    if (_currentHttpTask != null)
    {
        _currentHttpTask.AsAsyncOperation().Cancel();
    }

    if (_httpClient == null) _httpClient = new HttpClient();

    // Get the suggestions from an open search service.
    _currentHttpTask = _httpClient.GetStringAsync(url);
    string response = await _currentHttpTask;
    JsonArray parsedResponse = JsonArray.Parse(response);
    if (parsedResponse.Count > 1)
    {
        foreach (JsonValue value in parsedResponse[1].GetArray())
        {
            suggestions.AppendQuerySuggestion(value.GetString());
            if (suggestions.Size >= 5)
            {
                break;
            }
        }
    }
}
```

Let's walk through the code. We start off by checking if there's a task in progress, and if there is, we cancel it. Afterward a new instance of HttpClient gets declared. We then call the GetStringAsync method from the HttpClient class. What this does is send a GET request to the URL that's passed in as a parameter. The response it gets is serialized into a string. Notice the await keyword makes another appearance here, everything that makes a connection to an external service needs to be asynchronous, remember? The response is parsed into a JSON array, which is enumerated, and the first five are passed to the suggestion list. All of that code should produce the results shown in Figure 5-10.

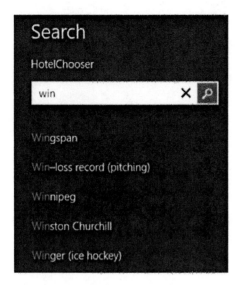

Figure 5-10. *OpenSearch suggestions*

Share Charm

The second charm we're going to take a look at is the Share charm, which provides a way for applications to talk to one another or to leverage one another's possibilities by sharing specific pieces of information. You can, for example, create a great drawing in a painting app and share it with the world using the Share charm and your favorite Twitter client or share a really interesting article with a friend through e-mail. Or you can have an app do an inventory count, and when you're finished, you use the Share charm to send the results to the back-end application. There are plenty of possible scenarios, and this shows how useful a uniform way of sharing information can be. The share contract supports sharing of text, links, HTML, images, storage files, and custom data. Let's take a look at them.

Sharing Text

Let's start off easy by sharing some text. We're still going to use our hotel app, this time to share a hotel experience with friends. The first big difference with the Search charm is that the Share charm can differ per page in the application. Our hotel app has two pages: a MainPage and a DetailPage. The app will only be able to share from the DetailPage. If we try to share from the MainPage, we'll get the results shown in Figure 5-11.

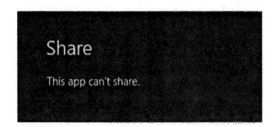

Figure 5-11. *Share charm*

Let's modify our DetailPage.xaml.cs to get some sharing going. First off we need a DataTransferManager. That's the class that takes care of all the sharing for us. The sharing itself happens with some help from Windows. When we click the Share charm, Windows 8 will act as a broker. It will look at the content we want to share and check in its list of registered share targets which target can receive that type of data. All those apps will then be presented to us in a nice list. Next stop is getting the share information for the current page and attaching a handler to the DataRequested event. I usually do that in a separate method that I call from the page's constructor, using the code in Listing 5-15.

Listing 5-15. Loading the Datasource for Sharing

```
public void ShareSourceLoad()
{
    _dataTransferManager = DataTransferManager.GetForCurrentView();
    try
    {
        _dataTransferManager.DataRequested += new TypedEventHandler<DataTransferManager,
DataRequestedEventArgs>(DataRequested);
    }
    catch
    {
        // you could do some exception handling here
    }
}
```

And of course there's the DataRequested event handler, which is accomplished using the code in Listing 5-16.

Listing 5-16. DataRequested

```
private void DataRequested(DataTransferManager sender, DataRequestedEventArgs args)
{
    args.Request.Data.Properties.Title = "Share your experience";
    args.Request.Data.Properties.Description = "Share your hotel experience with your friends!";

    args.Request.Data.SetText("This hotel rocks!");
}
```

And that's all there's to it, well to the basics anyway! You should also think about error handling here. If we run the app, navigate to the DetailPage, and access the Share charm now, we should get a list of installed applications that are able to receive shared text, as shown in Figure 5-12. This usually includes mail clients, Twitter clients, and so on. This will produce the text sharing page, as shown in Figure 5-13.

Share
Share your experience
Share your hotel experience with your f...
E-mail
FeestdagenBE
Quick Note
Share Target C# sample
glƏƏk!

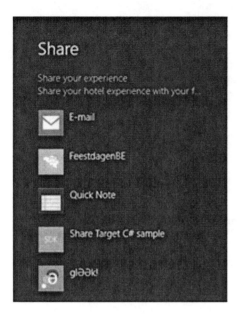

Figure 5-12. *Share contract*

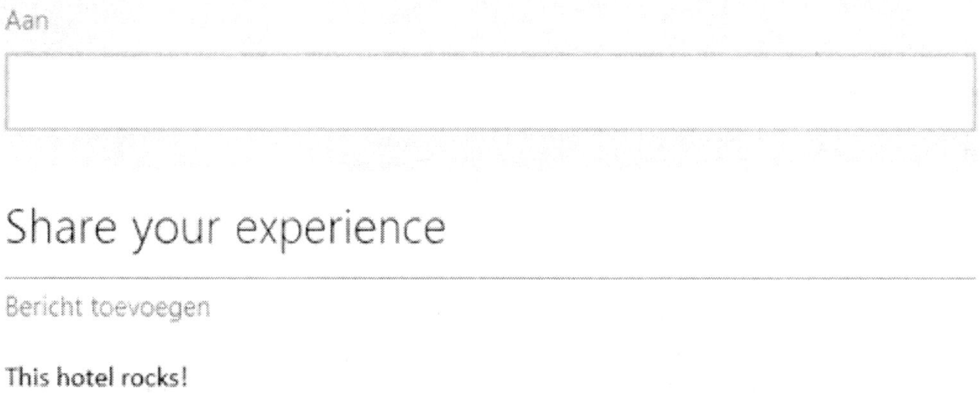
Aan
Share your experience
Bericht toevoegen
This hotel rocks!

Figure 5-13. *Share text*

That was surprisingly easy! Let's take it up a notch and share some links. Links aren't just text. They are interpreted by the share mechanism, and their page title and image are taken from the source and displayed in the share target.

Sharing Links

Sharing a link is not much different from sharing text. We're going to use the same event handler that we used for sharing text.

First, we need our link in the form of a URI. Next, we need to set the title and optionally the description of our share. And finally, to specify that we're sharing a link, we pass the URI to the `Request.Data`. Instead of passing in the URL of some hotel site, I'm using the Apress web site URL in Listing 5-17—they deserve some credit!

Listing 5-17. DataRequested Method

```
private void DataRequested(DataTransferManager sender, DataRequestedEventArgs args)
{
    Uri uri = new Uri(@"http://www.apress.com");
    args.Request.Data.Properties.Title = "The best book publisher in the world!";

    //optional
    //args.Request.Data.Properties.Description = "";
    args.Request.Data.SetUri(uri);
}
```

Now when we run the app, navigate to the detail page, and use the Share charm to create a new e-mail, we should get the results shown in Figure 5-14.

Aan

The best book publisher in the world!

Bericht toevoegen

Verstuurd vanuit Windows E-mail

Apress
http://www.apress.com/
Apress

Figure 5-14. Share links

Notice the arrows on the sides of the image? We can swipe through the available images on the site and send the one we really like. In this case, the default was a book cover from an iOS book, so I've quickly swiped to a more interesting subject.

Sharing links and text is easy and fast to set up. So now let's take a look at sharing HTML.

Sharing HTML

Why would we want to share HTML? Pretty easy—it allows us to do some mark up or to add a nice table to whatever we're sharing. Let's take, for example, an app for an inspector. He can do his inspection, note everything in the app, click the Share charm, and all his remarks are nicely bundled inside an HTML table so he can send it to the office without hassle. HTML provides for nice sharing, but do be careful! Let's say you want to share into an e-mail; keep in mind that not every e-mail client supports HTML e-mail, so think about whether this would be a real added value in your case.

This part won't take long. We're starting off the same way as the previous sharing parts, with an event handler and two lines of code, as shown in Listing 5-18.

Listing 5-18. DataRequested Method

```
private void DataRequested(DataTransferManager sender, DataRequestedEventArgs args)
{
    args.Request.Data.Properties.Title = "Share your experience";
    args.Request.Data.SetHtmlFormat(HtmlFormatHelper.CreateHtmlFormat("<h1>This hotel
rocks!</h1>"));
}
```

And that's basically it. The `HtmlFormatHelper` is a helper class in the Windows RT framework that sets all the correct headers in the HTML part so that it can be used in sharing and clipboard actions. Don't forget to add the `Title` or the sharing won't work. The results should look similar to those in Figure 5-15.

Aan

Share your experience

Bericht toevoegen

This hotel rocks!

Verstuurd vanuit Windows E-mail

Figure 5-15. *Share HTML*

Notice the large font? That's the `<H1>` tag doing its work. In the sample code that ships with this book, I've added an HTML table to the sample just to show how that would look. The results would look like those in Figure 5-16.

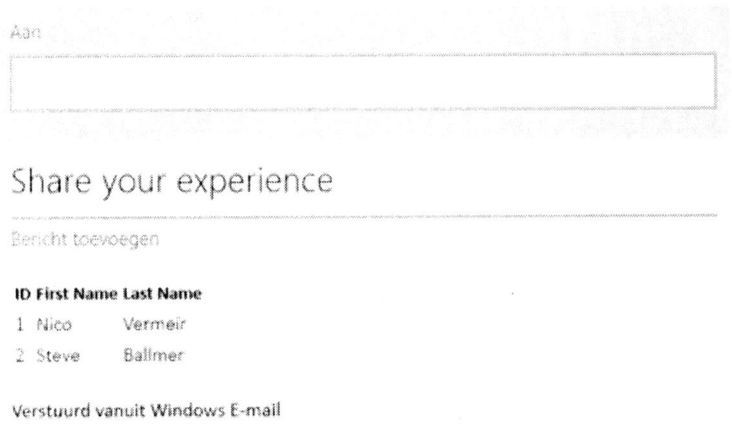

Aan

Share your experience

Bericht toevoegen

ID First Name Last Name

1 Nico   Vermeir

2 Steve   Ballmer

Verstuurd vanuit Windows E-mail

Figure 5-16. *Share HTML*

Pretty slick looking right? Let's have a look at sharing images next.

Sharing Images

Sharing images can be useful for a lot of reasons: sharing the latest action shots from your favorite hobby with the world on Facebook or Twitter or sending pictures from the construction site where you or your client is working for a house-building company, to give a few examples. What we're going to do in the hotel app is share an image of the hotel.

What we need to do is create a stream from the image and pass the stream into the DataRequested class. For the sake of readability, I've put the actual creation of the stream in a separate method, this is called separation of concerns, and you should always be doing this as well. Enough clean code preaching for now—let's share that image. We'll start with the event handler that we've gotten pretty familiar with, using the code in Listing 5-19.

Listing 5-19. DataRequested

```
private void DataRequested(DataTransferManager sender, DataRequestedEventArgs args)
{
    args.Request.Data.Properties.Title = "Share your experience";
    args.Request.Data.SetBitmap(SetImage());
}
```

If you've been reading this chapter from the beginning, then there shouldn't be any surprise in this. Now for the SetImage method, it takes the image from our solution in this case, but the image could also have come from the web or from the computer of the user, and it serializes it into a stream. That stream is what's passed into the SetBitmap method of the DataRequest. Create the stream using the code in Listing 5-20.

Listing 5-20. Create Stream from URI

```
private RandomAccessStreamReference SetImage()
{
    return RandomAccessStreamReference.CreateFromUri(new Uri(@"ms-appx:///Assets/hotel.jpg"));
}
```

If you've never encountered the `ms-appx///` notation, that's just a way to access the files inside your app package. The type of the file doesn't matter, it could be an image, a text file, a JSON file, and so on.

Now for the result of this image sharing. The e-mail client is not compatible with images, so it won't appear in the list when we click the Share charm. I took the Share Target app sample in Figure 5-17 from `dev.windows.com` (`http://code.msdn.microsoft.com/windowsapps/Sharing-Content-Target-App-e2689782`). It's perfectly possible that on your machine you'll see different apps appearing. I have an app installed that would take my image and turn it into a jigsaw puzzle.

Data Package Properties

Title: Share your experience

Description:

Data Package Content

Bitmap:

Figure 5-17. *Share target*

Sharing text, images, and HTML is all great and fun, but wouldn't it be nice if we could share our own POCO classes? Don't worry about that, I've saved the best for last. Sharing instances of your own classes can be done, but there are some caveats. Let's dive in and check it out.

Sharing Custom Data

What we need to set up to do a custom data share is a scheme so that the target app will recognize it correctly. Let's say we're sharing hotels through the Share charm but a competitor with a similar app is doing the same thing. It turns out the other app's hotel class has the same name as ours, but the properties are different. If the recognition is class-name based and we're using our app to share a hotel with the competitor's app, it just won't work. To fix that Windows RT relies on schemes for defining the data type. Microsoft recommends using a scheme from schema.org because those are widespread and well known. The complete list of schemas can be found at http://schema.org/docs/full.html. I would really recommend using one of the objects described there, because it makes for a uniform way of sharing. Take for example IMDb (International Movie Database). If they allow sharing of movie information and you have an app that can pick that share up, you can use the movie schema to define your movie class and it will pick up the IMDb share nicely.

Now on to our sample. There is a hotel schema at schema.org that is quite extensive and has a lot of other classes in it. For simplicity's sake, we'll only use the Name, Description, and PaymentsAccepted properties. For starters, we should expand our Hotel class a bit. But we have a stars property and a country property that are not in the schema. It is easiest here to just create a second class having only the properties that are in the schema. And to maintain clean code, we're going to have the Hotel class inherit from the new class, as shown in Listing 5-21.

Listing 5-21. Properties

```
public class HotelBase
{
    public string Name { get; set; }
    public string Description { get; set; }
    public string PaymentAccepted { get; set; }
}

public class Hotel : HotelBase
{
    public string Country { get; set; }
    public int Stars { get; set; }
}
```

The object itself needs to be serialized into JSON format with specific properties that define the type. That serialized string is then passed to the DataManager. The serialized object should look like the code in Listing 5-22.

Listing 5-22. JSON String

```
{
  "type" : "http://schema.org/Hotel",
  ""properties"" :
  {
      "name" : "Hotel 2"
  }
}
```

This is a pretty standard JSON object, as you can see. What we did is build a JSON string in code with a placeholder for the "properties" part, and the placeholder will get replaced by the serialized object, as in Listing 5-23. That should get us a JSON object similar to the one above.

Listing 5-23. JSON String with Placeholder for Class

```
private string _shareData =
        @"{
            ""type"" : ""http://schema.org/Hotel"",
```

```
        ""properties"" :
        %properties%
    }";
```

See the %properties%? That's the placeholder, and to replace it we use this piece of code:

```
_shareData = _shareData.Replace(@"%properties%", JsonConvert.SerializeObject(SelectedHotel));
```

You might not recognize the JsonConvert class. That one comes from Json.net, an open source library for all your JSON needs. It does quite a lot more and is way faster than the built-in serializer of .NET. You can easily add Json.net through NuGet (if you want to learn everything there is to learn about NuGet, I can highly recommend the book *Pro NuGet* written by two colleagues of mine and published by Apress). After this small commercial break, let's take a look at the complete code for sharing custom data, as shown in Listing 5-24.

Listing 5-24. Setting the Data

```
private string _shareData =
        @"{
            ""type"" : ""http://schema.org/Hotel"",
            ""properties"" :
            %properties%
        }";
private void DataRequested(DataTransferManager sender, DataRequestedEventArgs args)
{
    args.Request.Data.Properties.Title = "Share your experience";
    _shareData = _shareData.Replace(@"%properties%", JsonConvert.SerializeObject(SelectedHotel));
    args.Request.Data.SetData(@"http://schema.org/Hotel", _shareData);
}
```

And just like that, we're sharing custom information! A while ago an interesting library emerged for sharing custom data called Transhipment. All it does is give you an object that serializes correctly into the right format from a schema.org-defined object. At the time of writing, it does not include all schemas from the site, but since it's open source you can complete it if you like. I've taken the example from their web site, as shown in Listing 5-25, just to illustrate the difference between the manual way and the library way.

Listing 5-25. DataRequested Method

```
void DataRequested(DataTransferManager sender, DataRequestedEventArgs args)
{
    var request = args.Request;

    var geo = SchemaFactory.Create(Schema.GeoCoordinates) as IGeoCoordinates;
    geo.Name = "Polar Bear Provincial Park";
    geo.Latitude = "54.596931";
    geo.Longitude = "-83.283978";

    request.Data.Properties.Title = "Sample data";
    request.Data.Properties.Description = "data for " + geo.Type;
    request.Data.SetStructuredData(geo);
}
```

I think we've seen enough of this sharing stuff, let's take a look at the Settings charm.

Settings Charm

The Settings charm is usually used for, well, the settings, obviously. But it's also often used for access to the privacy policy or for support and contact information. By default, when you do nothing with the Search pane, it already has an option called Permissions and an option Rate and review (as shown in Figures 5-18 and 5-19) containing information of the capabilities of your app that are defined in the appxmanifest file. It also has sliders for specific capabilities like location access.

Figure 5-18. *Settings pane*

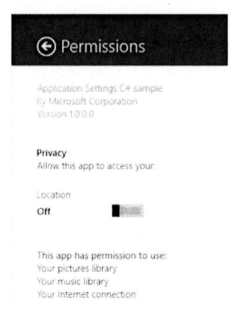

Figure 5-19. *Flyout example*

See how the Permissions pane looks? That control is called the flyout. It looks great and integrates very nicely with the Settings pane. The flyout control only has one problem, it's only available for JavaScript apps (but that's okay, they don't have strong typing so let them have this). Luckily for us there's always the open source community to count on fixing things. There a toolkit called Callisto floating around somewhere on the web, easily found through NuGet or at http://timheuer.github.com/callisto/, that provides us C# developers a flyout control. Let's start building our Settings pane and we'll also briefly explore the Callisto flyout control.

As with the other charms, the Settings charm also has its own class in the Windows RT framework. We need to call the GetForCurrentView() method once more and handle the CommandsRequested event. In that event handler, we declare the necessary commands we want to show in the Settings pane. Let's dive into the code.

First, we have the code for getting the pane for the current view part and registering the event handler, as shown in Listing 5-26.

Listing 5-26. Getting the SettingsPane

```
public MainPage()
{
    InitializeComponent();
    var searchPane = SearchPane.GetForCurrentView();
    searchPane.ShowOnKeyboardInput = true;

    SettingsPane.GetForCurrentView().CommandsRequested += BlankPage_CommandsRequested;

    LoadData();
}
```

And we also have the handler code, as shown in Listing 5-27.

Listing 5-27. CommandsRequested Handler

```
void BlankPage_CommandsRequested(SettingsPane sender, SettingsPaneCommandsRequestedEventArgs args)
{

    SettingsCommand cmd = new SettingsCommand("privacy", "Privacy Policy", x =>
Windows.System.Launcher.LaunchUriAsync(new Uri(@"http://www.spikie.be/win8/postcodes.html")));

    args.Request.ApplicationCommands.Add(cmd);
}
```

To explain this, let's take a look at the constructor parameters for the SettingsCommand class:

```
public SettingsCommand(object settingsCommandId, string label, UICommandInvokedHandler handler)
```

The first parameter is an ID, just give it a unique identifier. The second is the label, meaning how it will show up in the Settings pane. And the third is the event handler for when the command is invoked. The example I've used here is the code for navigating to a web page containing the privacy policy for one of my apps. The settings pane should look like the image in Figure 5-20.

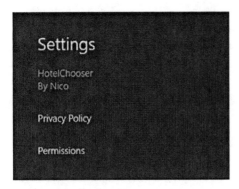

Figure 5-20. *Permissions option*

When the Privacy Policy command is clicked, the browser will open and the policy will appear. We will discuss the privacy policy in more detail in the Chapter 11, but for now just remember that as soon as your app makes an Internet connection, you will need to have a privacy policy in place.

Next, let's take a look at that flyout control in the Callisto toolkit. Start with adding the toolkit to your solution through NuGet, as shown in Figure 5-21.

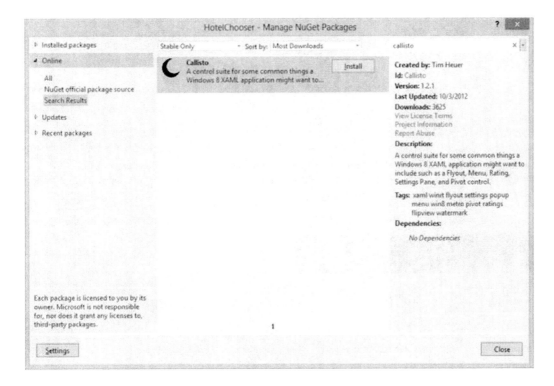

Figure 5-21. *Callisto on NuGet*

Next, I like to build the application to see if everything is in order. Once that checks out, we'll modify the Privacy Policy command from the previous step using the code in Listing 5-28 in order to show the privacy policy in the app rather than navigating away from the app into the browser. This should provide for a better user experience.

Listing 5-28. Creating Callisto flyout

```
void BlankPage_CommandsRequested(SettingsPane sender, SettingsPaneCommandsRequestedEventArgs args)
{

    SettingsCommand cmd = new SettingsCommand("privacy", "Privacy Policy", x => {
        // create a new instance of the flyout
        SettingsFlyout settings = new SettingsFlyout();

        //default is Narrow
        settings.FlyoutWidth = SettingsFlyout.SettingsFlyoutWidth.Wide;
        settings.Background = new SolidColorBrush(Colors.White);

        //header and content background
        settings.HeaderBrush = new SolidColorBrush(Colors.DarkRed);
        settings.HeaderText = "Privacy Policy";

        //logo
        BitmapImage bmp = new BitmapImage(new Uri("ms-appx:///Assets/hotel.jpg"));
        settings.SmallLogoImageSource = bmp;

        // open it
        settings.IsOpen = true;
    });

    args.Request.ApplicationCommands.Add(cmd);
}
```

Callisto basically provides us with two sizes for the flyout: Wide and Narrow. Furthermore, we can set the background color for both the body and the header of the control as well as a logo that will appear in the right corner of the pane. The results look like those shown in Figure 5-22.

Figure 5-22. *Callisto flyout*

Looks like the real deal! Thanks to Callisto, we can now use more or less the same flyout control that the JavaScript users have. You should of course add some controls to this pane, but that's a bit outside the scope of this book. Callisto is build by Tim Heuer and is available on GitHub, together with a very extensive documentation. Should you want to check it out, be sure to read through the documentation, as it is a big help. Here's the complete list of functionality in the Callisto toolkit at the time of writing.

The available controls are:

- Flyout

- Menu

- SettingsFlyout

- LiveTile

- Rating

- FlipViewIndicator

- DynamicTextBlock

- WatermarkTextBox

- TiltEffect

The available converters are:

- BooleanToVisibilityConverter

- BrushToColorConverter

- DateTimeFormatHelper

- LengthToBooleanConverter

- RelativeTimeConverter

The available extensions and helpers are:

- WebViewExtension

- Various Extension methods

- OAuth Helper

Summary

This chapter introduced us to charms and explained the way they make actions like searching, sharing information between apps, and settings uniform work throughout the entire operating system. The ease of use of these charms means that developers have no excuse not to use them in their apps. Users of Windows 8 will become accustomed to using these charms, and your apps will give a bad user experience if they don't follow the guidelines for these charms.

The Search charm is added just by adding a new file to the project, and this template is available in Visual Studio 2012. Almost all the code is available to use, so the only thing we need to do ourselves is add the search and filter logic to the page. If you have a pretty large amount of data, consider using the filters to make it easier for your users to find the exact data they're searching for.

The Share charm can be different for every page in the application, if you want it can even differ depending on what's available on the page. We call the GetForCurrentView method, handle the datarequested event, and set the title and description properties. After that, it's only a matter of specifying the type of data we want to share (text, URL, image, custom data), passing in the data themselves, and then allowing Windows to search your system for apps that can receive those specific types of data and providing the user with a nice list of those apps. The user then selects the one he or she likes and our data are "automagically" passed into that app.

The Settings charm works a lot like the Share charm. We also need to call the GetForCurrentView method. We then define one or more SettingsCommands passing in an ID, label, and event handler. If we need a flyout control, we can count on the open source Callisto toolkit to provide one or we can build our own control, because the framework doesn't provide a built-in flyout control for us poor C# developers.

The next chapter will walk you through the process of building and using live tiles.

CHAPTER 6

■ ■ ■

Using Live Tiles

Live tiles are a feature where the Windows platform, on Windows 8, Windows Phone, and Xbox, really shines. They provide information to users without them having to open each and every app. A quick glance at the Start screen is enough to know if new e-mails have arrived or to check if apps need updates or how their favorite team performed yesterday. It's up to the developer to leverage this functionality, and a good implementation of these notifications can really make an app stand out from the crowd.

But there's more to live tiles than just a way to provide certain information without opening the app. There's also a little something called secondary tiles. While the primary tile, or application tile as it's called, provides the main entry point to an app, the secondary tile is a hook to a certain page of the app. For example, in a sports app, we could allow our users to pin their favorite sports team to the Windows 8 Start screen so that with one tap on the secondary tile they could navigate to all stats and results of their favorite team instead of having to open the app, navigate to teams, and select the team there. Making the secondary tiles live tiles also makes it easy for users to keep track of multiple team results, even while the team is in the middle of a game.

Also in Windows 8, apps can have two sizes of tiles. There's a square and a rectangle about double the width of the square. We can choose whether our app supports both tile sizes, and it's up to the users which tile is actually used on their system (try right-clicking one of these tiles, and you'll see the option of using small or large tiles if it's an app that supports both). Let's take a look at how to implement and update tiles.

Application Tile

We'll begin with the application tile. This is a tile that every app has. By default, it has no live functionality, so we'll need to implement that ourselves. The application tile is the tile that shows up on your Start screen whenever you install an application, be it from Visual Studio, the Windows Store, or another source. Every app has it, and it always is the main entry point in the application.

Build Your Own Live Tile

Okay, time to build our own live tile. We'll start by creating a new empty application. The application will, for now, just have a text box and a button. When the button gets pressed, the text in the text box will be set as inner text for the live tile. The XAML for the MainPage is provided in Listing 6-1. The results will look like that shown in Figure 6-1.

Listing 6-1. XAML Snippet

```
<StackPanel Grid.Row="1" Margin="127, 0, 0, 0">
    <TextBox HorizontalAlignment="Left" Margin="0,10,0,0" TextWrapping="Wrap"
Text="{Binding TileMessage, Mode=TwoWay}" VerticalAlignment="Top" Width="352"/>
    <Button Content="Set app tile message" Click="Button_Click_1" HorizontalAlignment="Left"
VerticalAlignment="Top" Margin="0,20,0,0" Grid.Row="1" Height="73" Width="352"/>
</StackPanel>
```

Figure 6-1. *Setting a tile text*

This is pretty basic, there is a standard StackPanel in the second row of the grid that spans the entire page. Inside that StackPanel sits a text box and a button, the text box is bound to a property called TileMessage that sits in the code behind the page. The DataContext of this XAML page is set like this:

```
DataContext="{Binding RelativeSource={RelativeSource Self}}"
```

The property in the code behind the file is just a simple string:

```
public string TileMessage { get; set; }
```

The Button Click

As you can see, the button's Click event is being handled as well. In that event handler we'll set the text to our live tile. Let's have a look at the code, as provided in Listing 6-2.

Listing 6-2. Update Button Event

```
private void Button_Click_1(object sender, Windows.UI.Xaml.RoutedEventArgs e)
{
    UpdateTile(TileUpdateManager.GetTemplateContent(TileTemplateType. TileSquareBlock));
}

private void UpdateTile(XmlDocument tileXml)
{
    XmlNodeList tileTextAttributes = tileXml.GetElementsByTagName("text");

    if (tileTextAttributes.Count > 0)
    {
        tileTextAttributes[0].InnerText = TileMessage;
    }

    TileNotification tileNotification = new TileNotification(tileXml);
    TileUpdateManager.CreateTileUpdaterForApplication().Update(tileNotification);
}
```

The first thing we'll need to do is retrieve the desired template. We do this by calling the GetTemplateContent method on the TileUpdateManager class. Windows 8 has a bunch of templates, ranging from text-only templates to tiles that switch between images and text. The complete list consists of square tiles, wide tiles, and live tiles. The entire list, with examples, can be found at http://msdn.microsoft.com/library/windows/apps/Hh761491.

The templates themselves are built with XML. In this example app, we're using the `TileSquareBlock` template, which would use the code presented in Listing 6-3.

Listing 6-3. XML Snippet

```xml
<tile>
  <visual>
    <binding template="TileSquareBlock">
      <text id="1">Text Field 1</text>
      <text id="2">Text Field 2</text>
    </binding>
  </visual>
</tile>
```

The template speaks for itself. There are two text fields, the first one will show a large text with the second one underneath in a smaller font.

Now back to the code. We have to get our template from the `TileUpdateManager` class, and since we know what the template looks like, we can easily manipulate it using XML classes. First, we retrieve all "text" elements in the XML class (that's two objects in our case), then we take the first item in the list and set its inner text to the `TileMessage` property that is bound to the text box. Now that the template XML contains the text we want to show on the tile, we need to create a `TileNotification`. The `TileNotification` class constructor takes the XML as its parameter. To finish off, we need a `TileUpdater`. We can get an instance of that class by calling `CreateTileUpdaterForApplication` on the `TileUpdateManager`. Every instance of `TileUpdater` is bound to a specific tile, and that instance can only update that one tile to which it is bound. Interestingly enough, this is where a constructor overload takes in an app ID as its parameter, allowing us to update other app's tiles from our own app. Let's try it out. Run the app, enter a word in the text block, and click the button, then check the tile on the Start screen. It should look like the screen shown in Figure 6-2.

Figure 6-2. *Live tile*

That seems to work rather nicely! Remember, that second text element in the template? Let's check that one out. Create a second text box in the XAML and bind it to `SmallerMessage`, using the code in Listing 6-4. Then, in the code behind, create a second property using the code in Listing 6-5.

Listing 6-4. XAML Snippet

```
<StackPanel Grid.Row="1" Margin="127, 0, 0, 0">
    <TextBox HorizontalAlignment="Left" Margin="0,10,0,0" TextWrapping="Wrap" Text="{Binding
TileMessage, Mode=TwoWay}" VerticalAlignment="Top" Width="352"/>
    <TextBox HorizontalAlignment="Left" Margin="0,10,0,0" TextWrapping="Wrap" Text="{Binding
SmallerMessage, Mode=TwoWay}" VerticalAlignment="Top" Width="352"/>
    <Button Content="Set app tile message" Click="Button_Click_1" HorizontalAlignment="Left"
VerticalAlignment="Top" Margin="0,20,0,0" Grid.Row="1" Height="73" Width="352"/>
</StackPanel>
```

Listing 6-5. Code Behind

```
public string TileMessage { get; set; }
public string SmallerMessage { get; set; }

public MainPage()
{
    this.InitializeComponent();

    InitializeControls();
}

private void InitializeControls()
{
    TileMessage = "Enter tile message";
    SmallerMessage = "Enter smaller message";
}
```

We've set some initial values to the properties, and these will show up in the text boxes when the app launches. Next, we need to update the UpdateTile method so that it can set the second text element as well, using the code in Listing 6-6. To keep the method generic, we'll check for the amount of text elements that are found and set them accordingly.

Listing 6-6. UpdateTile Method

```
private void UpdateTile(XmlDocument tileXml)
{
    XmlNodeList tileTextAttributes = tileXml.GetElementsByTagName("text");

    if (tileTextAttributes.Count == 1)
    {
        tileTextAttributes[0].InnerText = TileMessage;
    }
    else if (tileTextAttributes.Count == 2)
    {
        tileTextAttributes[0].InnerText = TileMessage;
        tileTextAttributes[1].InnerText = SmallerMessage;
    }

    TileNotification tileNotification = new TileNotification(tileXml);
    TileUpdateManager.CreateTileUpdaterForApplication().Update(tileNotification);
}
```

Run the app, which should now produce the results shown in Figure 6-3.

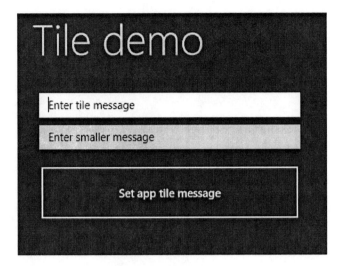

Figure 6-3. *The app user interface*

Enter some text, click the button, and check out your brand new tile, showing both messages, as shown in Figure 6-4.

Figure 6-4. *Live tile with two messages*

Congratulations! You've just build your first live tile! Let's jazz it a bit by also showing images instead of just text.

Live Tile with Image

The first thing we'll need to do in order to show images on our application tile is produce another template, and the template of choice is the `TileSquarePeekImageAndText01` template. Listing 6-7 supplies its XML coding.

Listing 6-7. XML Template

```
<tile>
  <visual>
    <binding template="TileSquarePeekImageAndText01">
      <image id="1" src="image1" alt="alt text"/>
      <text id="1">Text Header Field 1</text>
      <text id="2">Text Field 2</text>
      <text id="3">Text Field 3</text>
      <text id="4">Text Field 4</text>
    </binding>
  </visual>
</tile>
```

The text element with id="1" is the same large text as in the previous example, and the other three are all small text blocks stacked on top of each other. The image element takes in a string to an image path, so the image will slide up and down together with the text. Figure 6-5 shows a really cool book icon that we can place on our tile along with some text that, once again, can be set from inside the demo application.

Figure 6-5. *Tile icon*

So that you can include that image in the project, I have placed it inside the Assets folder for this book, but feel free to put it wherever you want. Just make sure that it's included in the project and remember where you have put it. The process to get this template to work is very similar to the previous one, we just set the text to the text elements we want (I'm only using two text elements in this example, but feel free to use all four) and set the image element to the path of the image. The code provided in Listing 6-8 will get you there.

Listing 6-8. UpdateTile with Support for Image

```
private void UpdateTile(XmlDocument tileXml)
{
    XmlNodeList tileTextAttributes = tileXml.GetElementsByTagName("text");

    if (tileTextAttributes.Count == 1)
    {
        tileTextAttributes[0].InnerText = TileMessage;
    }
```

```
    else if (tileTextAttributes.Count == 2)
    {
        tileTextAttributes[0].InnerText = TileMessage;
        tileTextAttributes[1].InnerText = SmallerMessage;
    }
    else //more then 2 text elements means we can set an image in this example
    {
        tileXml.GetElementsByTagName("image")[0].Attributes[1].InnerText =
"ms-appx:///Assets/icon.png";
        tileTextAttributes[0].InnerText = TileMessage;
        tileTextAttributes[1].InnerText = SmallerMessage;
    }

    TileNotification tileNotification = new TileNotification(tileXml);
    TileUpdateManager.CreateTileUpdaterForApplication().Update(tileNotification);
}
```

As the comment in this code points out, as soon as our demo app detects more than two text elements, it assumes it's the TileSquarePeekImageAndText01 template that's getting used. The path to the image is set as an ms-appx resource, remember that one? We've used it before when we discussed the charms, it points to a resource embedded in the app package. Also for the image we need to retrieve the src attribute instead of directly setting the value to the element. According to the template, src is the second attribute, with id being the first one. Because we're using zero indexing, the second attribute has index 1. For the XAML part, I've modified the application to show a second StackPanel with the image and the same two text boxes from the first part of this chapter, with the same bindings, as shown in Listing 6-9.

Listing 6-9. New StackPanel

```
<StackPanel Grid.Row="1" Margin="26,0,482,363" Grid.Column="1">
    <Image Height="109" Source="Assets/icon.png"/>
    <TextBox HorizontalAlignment="Left" Margin="0,10,0,0" TextWrapping="Wrap" Text="{Binding
TileMessage, Mode=TwoWay}" VerticalAlignment="Top" Width="352"/>
    <TextBox HorizontalAlignment="Left" Margin="0,10,0,0" TextWrapping="Wrap" Text="{Binding
SmallerMessage, Mode=TwoWay}" VerticalAlignment="Top" Width="352"/>
    <Button Content="Set app tile message &amp; image" Click="Button_Click_2"
HorizontalAlignment="Left" VerticalAlignment="Top" Margin="0,20,0,0" Grid.Row="1" Height="73"
Width="352"/>
</StackPanel>
```

The only difference is the image control and the button, which has another event handler that basically does the same as the first one but gets the TileSquarePeekImageAndText01 template instead of the TileSquareBlock template. Listing 6-10 provides the code for calling the UpdateTile method. Figure 6-6 is the results of implementing these steps.

Listing 6-10. Calling the UpdateTile Method

```
private void Button_Click_2(object sender, Windows.UI.Xaml.RoutedEventArgs e)
{
    UpdateTile(TileUpdateManager.GetTemplateContent(TileTemplateType.TileSquarePeekImageAndText01));
}
```

Figure 6-6. *Steps in the live tile*

Feel free to experiment with different templates until you find the one that best suits your needs. Also try to implement your live tiles in both the square and the wide size to determine which gives the best experience to your users.

Secondary Tiles

Okay, so we have a live tile, that's cool. Now let's take a look at secondary tiles. We'll put the settings for the secondary tile on another page, and the tile itself will open that page when clicked. Let's add a second basic page to the project, which we will call SecondaryTilePage.

Adding a Secondary Tile

In that new page, I've copied the StackPanel with the image, two text boxes, and the button from the MainPage. We need to also create another image for the tile so we can tell the difference between the application tile and the secondary tile. Listing 6-11 presents the XAML code to do this.

Listing 6-11. XAML Snippet

```
<StackPanel Grid.Row="1" Margin="26,0,482,363" Grid.Column="1">
    <Image Height="109" Source="Assets/secondaryIcon.png"/>
    <TextBox HorizontalAlignment="Left" Margin="0,10,0,0" TextWrapping="Wrap"
Text="{Binding TileMessage, Mode=TwoWay}" VerticalAlignment="Top" Width="352"/>
    <TextBox HorizontalAlignment="Left" Margin="0,10,0,0" TextWrapping="Wrap"
Text="{Binding SmallerMessage, Mode=TwoWay}" VerticalAlignment="Top" Width="352"/>
    <Button Content="Set app tile message &amp; image" Click="Button_Click_2"
HorizontalAlignment="Left" VerticalAlignment="Top" Margin="0,20,0,0" Grid.Row="1" Height="73"
Width="352"/>
</StackPanel>
```

The new icon is basically the same book icon, except it has a green background instead of blue. Don't forget to add a way to navigate to this page! I've placed a simple button on the MainPage with this code attached to the Click event:

```
Frame.Navigate(typeof (SecondaryTilePage));
```

On the SecondaryTilePage, we have everything we need to update a secondary tile but nothing to create one. We must add another button to that page for this purpose. The code in Listing 6-12 will create that secondary tile.

Listing 6-12. Creating a Secondary Tile

```
private void Button_Click_1(object sender, Windows.UI.Xaml.RoutedEventArgs e)
{
    SecondaryTile secondaryTile = new SecondaryTile(
                                    "tileId",
                                    "SecondTile",
                                    "Secondary Tile",
                                    "message=I was clicked!",
                                    TileOptions.ShowNameOnLogo,
                                    new Uri("ms-appx:///Assets/secondaryIcon.png"));

    secondaryTile.RequestCreateAsync();
}
```

▨ **Note** If you want to follow the Microsoft design guidelines, and you should, then creating a secondary tile is usually done from the AppBar. Try not to put buttons on this page as much as possible. Your content should be the main form of navigation, and all actions should be in the AppBars.

The SecondaryTile class is a class we get from the Windows 8 SDK. As a first parameter, it needs a unique ID to identify the secondary tile, and the second parameter is the short name for the tile followed by the display name. The fourth parameter is a string containing the arguments that are passed to the activated page when the secondary tile is clicked. Then there are some tile options, like the option to roam the secondary tile over devices, and it ends with a URI to the image. Once that instance is defined, we can call upon the RequestCreateAsync method from the SecondaryTile class. This method will show a pop-up to the user asking for permission to create the tile. When permission has been given, the tile is created and shows up on the Start screen, as shown in Figure 6-7.

SecondTile

Pin to Start

Figure 6-7. *Creating a secondary tile*

Adding Navigation to the Secondary Tile

Now we want this secondary tile to navigate to the SecondaryTilePage. In Windows RT development, this differs quite a bit from Windows Phone and is a bit more work, but it's also more powerful. First, we're going to adjust the arguments parameter, so replace the previous code with the code in Listing 6-13.

Listing 6-13. Creating the Tile

```
private void Button_Click_1(object sender, Windows.UI.Xaml.RoutedEventArgs e)
{
    SecondaryTile secondaryTile = new SecondaryTile(
                                        "tileId",
                                        "SecondTile",
                                        "Secondary Tile",
                                        "target=SecondaryTilePage",
                                        TileOptions.ShowNameOnLogo,
                                        new Uri("ms-appx:///Assets/secondaryIcon.png"));

    secondaryTile.RequestCreateAsync();
}
```

Did you notice the target=SecondaryTilePage? It is just a plain string, but it will get passed into the LaunchedEventArgs from the OnLaunched event on App.xaml. Now we need to interpret the arguments in that same event handler. We first check if there are any arguments passed that contain "target=", and if there are, we just navigate to the SecondaryTilePage because in our example there's only one alternate page to which we can navigate. In a bigger application, we would need to check the name passed in the arguments and navigate to the corresponding page. Listing 6-14 provides the code to receive this argument.

Listing 6-14. Receiving Arguments from Secondary Tile

```
protected override void OnLaunched(LaunchActivatedEventArgs args)
{
    Frame rootFrame = Window.Current.Content as Frame;

    // Do not repeat app initialization when the Window already has content,
    // just ensure that the window is active
    if (rootFrame == null)
    {
        // Create a Frame to act as the navigation context and navigate to the first page
        rootFrame = new Frame();

        if (args.PreviousExecutionState == ApplicationExecutionState.Terminated)
        {
            //TODO: Load state from previously suspended application
        }

        // Place the frame in the current Window
        Window.Current.Content = rootFrame;

        if (args.Arguments.Contains("target="))
        {
            rootFrame.Navigate(typeof (SecondaryTilePage));
        }
    }

    if (rootFrame.Content == null)
    {
        // When the navigation stack isn't restored navigate to the first page,
        // configuring the new page by passing required information as a navigation
        // parameter
        if (!rootFrame.Navigate(typeof(MainPage), args.Arguments))
        {
            throw new Exception("Failed to create initial page");
        }
    }
    // Ensure the current window is active
    Window.Current.Activate();
}
```

I've pasted the entire function here as a reference, but make sure to put your navigation logic after `Window.Current.Content = rootFrame` or your navigation won't work.

Updating a Secondary Tile

Let's get our secondary tile to update. This part of the chapter is actually 99 percent code reuse from updating the application tile. The only difference is that we need to verify there actually is a secondary tile. The coding needed for the button click event is presented in Listing 6-15.

Listing 6-15. Updating a Secondary Tile

```
private void Button_Click_2(object sender, RoutedEventArgs e)
{
    if (SecondaryTile.Exists("tileId"))
    {

UpdateTile(TileUpdateManager.GetTemplateContent(TileTemplateType.TileSquarePeekImageAndText01));
    }
}
```

The .Exists method is part of the SecondaryTile class, which takes in the tile ID (the first parameter of the constructor when creating a secondary tile). If it already exists, we once again get an XML template and pass it into the UpdateTile function, which is very slightly modified, as shown in Listing 6-16.

Listing 6-16. UpdateTile Method

```
private void UpdateTile(XmlDocument tileXml)
{
    XmlNodeList tileTextAttributes = tileXml.GetElementsByTagName("text");

    if (tileTextAttributes.Count == 1)
    {
        tileTextAttributes[0].InnerText = TileMessage;
    }
    else if (tileTextAttributes.Count == 2)
    {
        tileTextAttributes[0].InnerText = TileMessage;
        tileTextAttributes[1].InnerText = SmallerMessage;
    }
    else //more then 2 text elements means we can set an image in this example
    {
        tileXml.GetElementsByTagName("image")[0].Attributes[1].InnerText = "ms-appx:///Assets/
secondaryIcon.png";
        tileTextAttributes[0].InnerText = TileMessage;
        tileTextAttributes[1].InnerText = SmallerMessage;
    }

    TileNotification tileNotification = new TileNotification(tileXml);
    TileUpdateManager.CreateTileUpdaterForSecondaryTile("tileId").Update(tileNotification);
}
```

The last line of code is the only difference here, and it now creates an updater for a secondary tile. It needs the tile ID as a parameter, so the tile update that gets created there is bound to that specific tile and will only be able to update that specific tile.

If we would ever need to update all secondary tiles, there's a way to enumerate and change them all. Listing 6-17 provides the code, but I have commented in its use, so feel free to try it.

Listing 6-17. Updating All Secondary Tiles

```
private async void UpdateAllSecondaryTiles()
{
    IReadOnlyList<SecondaryTile> tilelist = await SecondaryTile.FindAllAsync();

    foreach (var tile in tilelist)
    {
UpdateTile(TileUpdateManager.GetTemplateContent(TileTemplateType.TileSquarePeekImageAndText01),
tile.TileId);
    }
}
```

First, get all tiles working asynchronously, enumerate them, and then call the update method each time, passing in the template and the tile ID.

Badges

With all of this information in place, let's finish this chapter with a discussion on badges. *Badges* are small notifications on your tiles that either show a number or a glyph. Most Twitter applications use badges to notify how many tweets you have received.

Creating a badge is quite similar to creating an actual live tile. We first need to get the XML scheme for either a number or a glyph, set the value, and then call an updater. The XML scheme of a badge only has one element: <badge>. A full list of values can be found on MSDN (http://msdn.microsoft.com/en-us/library/windows/apps/br212849.aspx). Table 6-1 shows the available values for glyphs.

Table 6-1. *Available Glyphs*

Status	Glyph	XML
None	No badge shown	<badge value="none"/>
Activity	↻	<badge value="activity"/>
Alert	＊	<badge value="alert"/>
Available	◯	<badge value="available"/>
Away	●	<badge value="away"/>
Busy	◎	<badge value="busy"/>
New message	✉	<badge value="newMessage"/>
Paused	❚❚	<badge value="paused"/>

(continued)

Table 6-1. (*continued*)

Status	Glyph	XML
Playing	▶	`<badge value="playing"/>`
Unavailable	◉	`<badge value="unavailable"/>`
Error	⊗	`<badge value="error"/>`
Attention	❗	`<badge value="attention"/>`

Building the Badges

Let's dive into some code. I've created another function, just like when we were creating live tiles, only this time for setting badges. Listing 6-18 provides the code you need to accomplish this.

Listing 6-18. Creating a Badge

```
private void Button_Click_4(object sender, Windows.UI.Xaml.RoutedEventArgs e)
{
    SetBadge(BadgeUpdateManager.GetTemplateContent(BadgeTemplateType.BadgeNumber));
}

private void SetBadge(XmlDocument template)
{
    XmlElement textnode = (XmlElement)template.SelectSingleNode("/badge");

    textnode.SetAttribute("value", BadgeNumber);

    BadgeNotification badgeNotification = new BadgeNotification(template);

    BadgeUpdateManager.CreateBadgeUpdaterForApplication().Update(badgeNotification);
}
```

We're using BadgeUpdateManger this time, but this class works pretty much the same as the TileUpdateManager. In the SetBadge function, we set the value attribute to the BadgeNumber property, which is just another string property like the ones used to set the text to the tiles. The XAML coding is provided in Listing 6-19.

Listing 6-19. XAML Snippet

```
<StackPanel Grid.Column="2" HorizontalAlignment="Left" Height="178" Margin="10,10,0,0" Grid.Row="1"
VerticalAlignment="Top" Width="298">
    <TextBox TextWrapping="Wrap" Text="{Binding BadgeNumber, Mode=TwoWay}"/>
    <Button Content="Set number" HorizontalAlignment="Stretch" VerticalAlignment="Stretch"
Margin="0,20,0,0" Click="Button_Click_4"/>
    <Button Content="Set glyph" HorizontalAlignment="Stretch" VerticalAlignment="Stretch"
Margin="0,20,0,0"/>
</StackPanel>
```

Don't forget to set that text box's binding to TwoWay, no surprises here. Run the app, fill in some number, and check out the application tile, as shown in Figure 6-8.

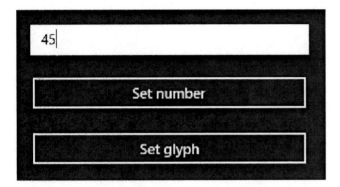

Figure 6-8. *The app user interface for adding badges*

We have two buttons here, as shown in Figure 6-8. The top one is the one we've just implemented. When we click it, the result will look like the image in Figure 6-9.

Figure 6-9. *Tile with badge*

Now that's a nice little badge! One small caveat about badges though. They can only handle two digits. Figure 6-10 shows how it looks when we try to set a number higher than 99 to a badge.

Figure 6-10. *A badge can't go higher than 99*

It is a somewhat elegant solution to a problem. Try to show your users the correct number once they launch the app.

Let's try to set a glyph next. Listing 6-20 presents the code for the second button.

Listing 6-20. Setting a glyph

```
private void Button_Click_5(object sender, Windows.UI.Xaml.RoutedEventArgs e)
{
    BadgeNumber = "newMessage";

SetBadge(BadgeUpdateManager.GetTemplateContent(BadgeTemplateType.BadgeGlyph));
}
```

When the set glyph button is clicked, we set the property to "newMessage", which is one of the available values for glyphs (see Table 6-1). We then call the same function as before but pass in the BadgeGlyph template. Figure 6-11 shows the result.

Figure 6-11. *Live tile with glyph*

Now that's a sweet looking badge right there! Should you want to use badges on secondary tiles, all you need to do is replace this line:

```
BadgeUpdateManager.CreateBadgeUpdaterForApplication().Update(badgeNotification);
```

with this line:

```
BadgeUpdateManager.CreateBadgeUpdaterForSecondaryTile("tileId").Update(badgeNotification);
```

Updating Tiles

Let's wrap up this chapter by looking at the different methods of updating your tiles, either through the notification queue or by using background tasks.

Notification Queues

Tiles can make use of notification queues. *Notification queues* can contain up to five notifications at the same time, and the live tile will cycle through them and show them one at a time. If a sixth item is added to the queue, the first item is removed. To make use of notification queues, the only thing we need is this line of code:

```
TileUpdateManager.CreateTileUpdaterForApplication().EnableNotificationQueue(true);
```

Place that line of code in the constructor of your MainPage and the app will start queueing updates (maximum five, on a first-in, first-out principle). The order in which the updates are shown on the tile is not fixed. They may appear out of order. Should you want to remove specific notifications instead of letting the system deal with it, you can add tags to each notification, such as this one:

```
tileNotification.Tag = "stockMSFT";
```

That tag is an ID that's unique for this notification and makes it possible to find it by iterating over the notifications and checking for the tag.

Background Tasks

Background tasks are tasks that can execute even when your app is not running. They can do a variety of tasks, including updating your tiles. Let's have a look at how to do this. First, we need to add a project to our solution. Under Add New Project, we need to select Windows Runtime Component, as shown in Figure 6-12.

Figure 6-12. *Adding a Windows Runtime Component*

Once that's added, we need to create a class in that Runtime Component that implements the IBackgroundTask interface. Use the code in Listing 6-21 to do that.

Listing 6-21. Declaring a Background Task

```
public sealed class BgTask : IBackgroundTask
{
    public void Run(IBackgroundTaskInstance taskInstance)
    {
    }
}
```

The interface has one member, a method called Run. When the background task executes, it will run this method. To update our tiles from the background task, we need to place our already familiar code into the Run method, as provided in Listing 6-22.

Listing 6-22. Updating Tile from Background Task

```
public void Run(IBackgroundTaskInstance taskInstance)
{
    XmlDocument tileXml = TileUpdateManager.GetTemplateContent(TileTemplateType.
TileWideImageAndText01);
    XmlNodeList tileTextAttributes = tileXml.GetElementsByTagName("text");

    tileXml.GetElementsByTagName("image")[0].Attributes[1].InnerText = "ms-appx:///Assets/icon.png";

    tileTextAttributes[0].InnerText = "updated from background task";

    TileNotification tileNotification = new TileNotification(tileXml);
    TileUpdateManager.CreateTileUpdaterForApplication().Update(tileNotification);
}
```

With that, our background task is finished. Next, we need to go to our manifest file and set a declaration for a background task, as shown in Figure 6-13.

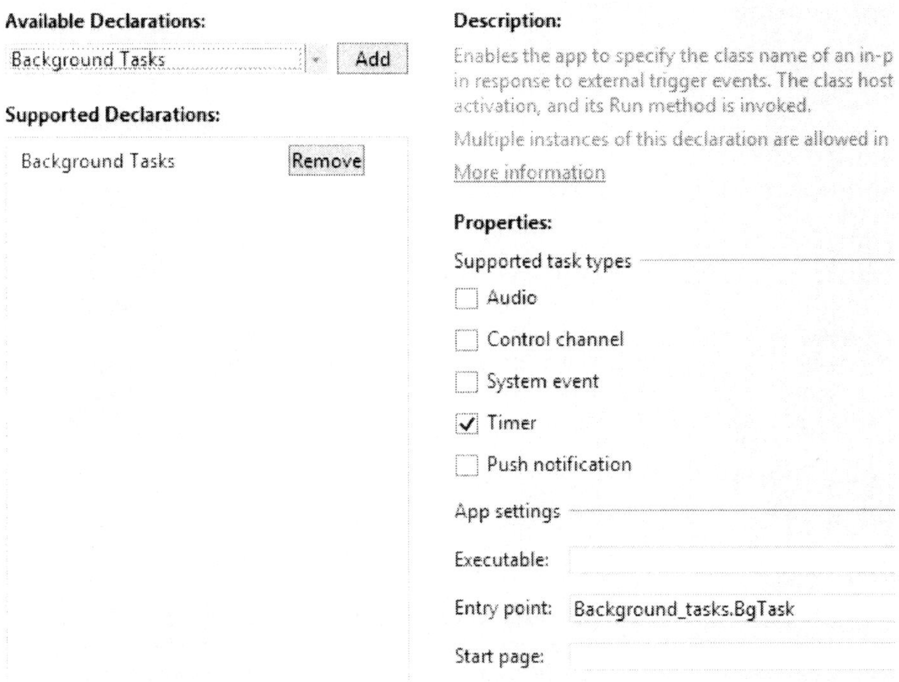

Available Declarations:

Background Tasks [▾] [Add]

Supported Declarations:

Background Tasks [Remove]

Description:

Enables the app to specify the class name of an in-p in response to external trigger events. The class host activation, and its Run method is invoked.

Multiple instances of this declaration are allowed in

More information

Properties:

Supported task types

☐ Audio

☐ Control channel

☐ System event

☑ Timer

☐ Push notification

App settings

Executable: [ ]

Entry point: [Background_tasks.BgTask]

Start page: [ ]

Figure 6-13. *Adding a declaration*

We're using a timer-based background task in this example. That means our task will run at fixed times. The last thing we need to do now is register our background task in the Windows operating system so that it can run without the application being active. Listing 6-23 presents that code.

Listing 6-23. Registering a Background Task

```
private void Button_RegisterTask(object sender, Windows.UI.Xaml.RoutedEventArgs e)
{
    var taskName = "BackgroundTask";
    bool taskRegistered = false;

    foreach (var task in BackgroundTaskRegistration.AllTasks)
    {
        if (task.Value.Name == taskName)
        {
            taskRegistered = true;
        }
    }

    if (taskRegistered) return; //task already registered

    var builder = new BackgroundTaskBuilder
                    {
                        Name = taskName,
                        TaskEntryPoint = "Background_tasks.BgTask"
                    };
```

```
builder.SetTrigger(new TimeTrigger(15, false));

builder.Register();
}
```

First, we need to give our background task a name, a unique ID that we use to identify it. Then we iterate through all registered tasks and check if the task that we want to register already exists. If it does, we set `taskRegistered` to true. If it exists, we exit the method because there's no use in registering it again. If it doesn't exist, we create a new instance of `BackgroundTaskBuilder` passing in the name that we've chosen at the start of the method and passing in the task entry point. That should be the fully qualified name of the background task class name (namespace plus class name). Since this is a timer background task, we need to set a trigger. The first parameter in the `TimeTrigger` constructor is the number of minutes between each run. Setting it lower than 15 minutes will throw an exception, so make sure to set it to at least 15 minutes. The second parameter determines if the trigger will only fire once or indeterminately. After that, we call the `Register` method on the `BackgroundTaskBuilder` instance to register the task with the operating system.

Before running this code, make sure that the app project references the background task project.

Debugging a Background Task

Debugging a background task can be tricky. Do we really have to wait at least 15 minutes every time we want to debug a timer background task? Luckily, Visual Studio 2012 has us covered. The only thing we need to do is set a breakpoint in the background task and run the application. With the app still running, return to Visual Studio and make sure that you have the Debug Location toolbar visible. Click the Suspend button and select Background Task, as shown in Figure 6-14. The task will run immediately and will break at the breakpoint that we've set.

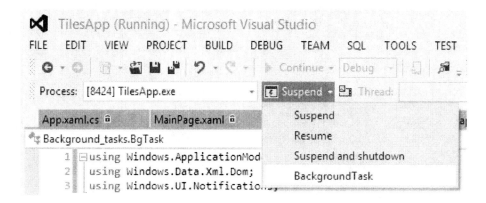

Figure 6-14. *Debugging a background task*

Background Task Triggers

Background tasks can also fire from triggers. Triggers fire whenever a certain event on the operating system level occurs, for example, when the state of the network connection changes or when a user logs on. Table 6-2 lists the `SystemTriggers`. To register a `SystemTrigger` instead of a `TimeTrigger`, use this code:

```
builder.SetTrigger(new SystemTrigger(SystemTriggerType.TimeZoneChange, false));
```

Table 6-2. *List of SystemTriggers*

Member	Value	description
Invalid | invalid	0	Not a valid trigger type.
SmsReceived | smsReceived	1	The background task is triggered when a new Short Message Service (SMS) message is received by an installed mobile broadband device.
UserPresent | userPresent	2	The background task is triggered when the user becomes present.
		Note An app must be placed on the lock screen before it can successfully register background tasks using this trigger type.
UserAway | userAway	3	The background task is triggered when the user becomes absent.
		Note An app must be placed on the lock screen before it can successfully register background tasks using this trigger type.
NetworkStateChange | networkStateChange	4	The background task is triggered when a network change occurs, such as a change in cost or connectivity.
ControlChannelReset | controlChannelReset	5	The background task is triggered when a control channel is reset.
		Note An app must be placed on the lock screen before it can successfully register background tasks using this trigger type.
InternetAvailable | internetAvailable	6	The background task is triggered when the Internet becomes available.
SessionConnected | sessionConnected	7	The background task is triggered when the session is connected.
		Note An app must be placed on the lock screen before it can successfully register background tasks using this trigger type.
ServicingComplete | servicingComplete	8	The background task is triggered when the system has finished updating an app.
LockScreenApplicationAdded | lockScreenApplicationAdded	9	The background task is triggered when a tile is added to the lock screen.
LockScreenApplicationRemoved | lockScreenApplicationRemoved	10	The background task is triggered when a tile is removed from the lock screen.
TimeZoneChange | timeZoneChange	11	The background task is triggered when the time zone changes on the device (for example, when the system adjusts the clock for daylight saving time).
OnlineIdConnectedStateChange | onlineIdConnectedStateChange	12	The background task is triggered when the Microsoft account connected to the account changes.

Summary

This chapter discussed live tiles and how they make the Windows platform unique. They provide a great way of showing information of all kinds to our users, requiring them to launch the app. The tiles also provide an opportunity for the developer to draw users back into the app. Social network applications can show the latest status updates from friends, and television show tracking applications can show air dates on a tile. I'm convinced that over 80 percent of all apps out there can benefit from using a live tile.

There are two kinds of tiles in Windows 8. There's the application tile that appears whenever an application is installed and can't be removed unless the user removes the entire app. Then there's the secondary tiles, which need to be set from code. The user needs to confirm that they really want a second tile on the Start screen. These secondary tiles also provide a hook into a certain part of the application, passing in certain arguments to launch a specific page, for example.

We've also discussed the use of badges. Badges are overlays on a tile. They work both on application tiles and on secondary tiles. Badges can show either a number (a maximum of two digits) or they can show a glyph. Badges are perfect for showing users that they have new messages or how many interesting articles just appeared on their newsfeed.

Last but not least, we've taken a look at the different methods of updating tiles: either through the notification queue or by using background tasks. Background tasks can run on fixed intervals or when certain system events occur, such as changing the network state.

Consider using tiles or badges in your application. They're easy to implement and make the overall experience of your apps feel much richer as the functionality expands outside the app and into the operating system itself.

The next chapter will look at the process of using notifications.

CHAPTER 7

Notifications

Windows 8 has lots of ways to notify the user of whatever is happening inside an app. There are the tiles, both application tiles and secondary tiles, there are badges that can show either glyphs or numbers, and then there are notifications. We've talked about the first two choices in Chapter 6, so in this chapter we'll discuss notifications. We're going to focus on toast notifications and lockscreen notifications.

Toast Notifications

The most common notification in Windows 8 is the toast notification. This kind of notification has become familiar in Windows Phone 7 and has now made its way to Redmond's new operating system. Since apps in Windows 8 are mostly asynchronous, the toasts provide a great way of notifying the user when an action completes. A great example of this are apps that track a collection. The user (or collector in this case) adds a bunch of items to his or her collection, clicks the Save button, and the app calls the save function asynchronously. The user can keep using the app or the computer in whatever way he or she wants, and the application will show a toast notification when the save task is completed. Figure 7-1 shows what a normal toast notification looks like.

Figure 7-1. *Toast message*

Toast notifications can contain text, titles, images, and even audio signals. Let's create some toast, the not eatable kind!

Building a Toast-Capable App

The very first thing we need to do is specify in the manifest file that this app is toast capable. Double-click the manifest file, in the Application UI tab, select All Image Assets and set Toast capable to Yes, as shown in Figure 7-2.

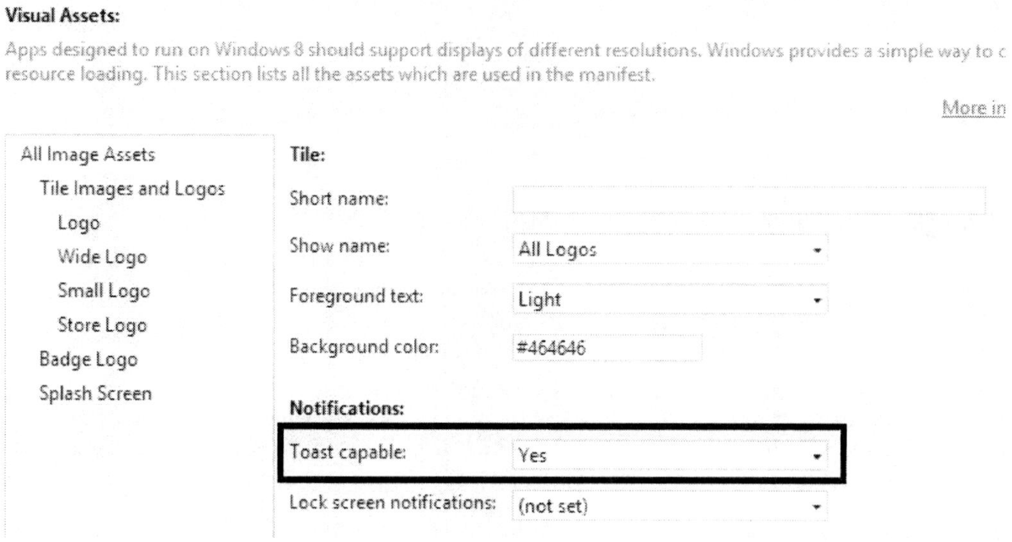

Visual Assets:

Apps designed to run on Windows 8 should support displays of different resolutions. Windows provides a simple way to c
resource loading. This section lists all the assets which are used in the manifest.

More in

All Image Assets	Tile:	
Tile Images and Logos	Short name:	
Logo	Show name:	All Logos
Wide Logo	Foreground text:	Light
Small Logo		
Store Logo	Background color:	#464646
Badge Logo		
Splash Screen	**Notifications:**	
	Toast capable:	Yes
	Lock screen notifications:	(not set)

Figure 7-2. *Toast capability in the manifest file*

Creating toast notifications is almost identical to creating live tiles. The templates are made up by some XML code. We need to set some elements and attributes in that template and push it to the ToastNotificationManager. Let's create a small app that produces these toasts. Create a new blank project and add the XAML snippet from Listing 7-1. The official notifications sample, which can be found on dev.windows.com, includes a nice library called NotificationExtensions that handles the XML content, so we can set everything in a more ".net way" (it's basically an interface-based wrapper around the XML templates). Feel free to check that out.

Listing 7-1. XAML Snippet

```
<Button Content="Show toast" HorizontalAlignment="Left" VerticalAlignment="Top" Margin="60,149,0,0"
Click="ButtonSendNotificationClick"/>
<TextBlock HorizontalAlignment="Left" Margin="10,10,0,0" TextWrapping="Wrap" Text="text toast"
VerticalAlignment="Top" Style="{StaticResource SubheaderTextStyle}" Width="308"/>
<TextBox x:Name="TextboxToastText" HorizontalAlignment="Left" TextWrapping="Wrap"
VerticalAlignment="Top" Margin="10,93,0,0" Width="272"/>
```

Figure 7-3 shows what this snippet should look like when it is run.

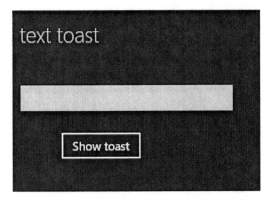

Figure 7-3. App UI

Let's have a look at the code behind the button, as presented in Listing 7-2.

Listing 7-2. Send the Notification

```
private void ButtonSendNotificationClick(object sender, RoutedEventArgs e)
{
    var notifier = ToastNotificationManager.CreateToastNotifier();
    var template = ToastNotificationManager.GetTemplateContent(ToastTemplateType.ToastText01);

    var element = template.GetElementsByTagName("text")[0];
    element.AppendChild(template.CreateTextNode(TextboxToastText.Text.Trim()));

    var toast = new ToastNotification(template);
    notifier.Show(toast);

}
```

First, we need to create a ToastNotifier. This is an object bound to this application (it can be bound to another application by adding the app ID as a parameter for the constructor) that will provide everything we need to get toasts. The ToastNotifier gets created by calling the CreateToastNotifier function of the ToastNotificationManager, a class sitting in the Windows.UI.Notifications namespace. The second thing we need is the template. Just like tiles, the toast notification is made up of an XML template describing the structure of the toast. For this first case, we're just using the simple text toast, and the XML code for this is provided in Listing 7-3.

Listing 7-3. XML Template

```
<toast>
    <visual>
        <binding template="ToastText01">
            <text id="1">bodyText</text>
        </binding>
    </visual>
</toast>
```

All we need to do is fill in the text element from code by first calling the GetElementsByTagName("text") function. That function returns an XmlNodeList with only one item in this case. We set the content of the text box to the value of that element and, last but not least, we need to create a ToastNotification pass in the modified template and call the Show method. Run the app, enter some text in the box, click the button, and watch magic happen right before your eyes. Well not really magic, but it's still pretty cool!

Toast Templates

The complete list of the eight toast templates is provided in Table 7-1.

Table 7-1. *XML Templates for Toasts*

Template name	XML snippet
ToastText01	```<toast>
<visual>
<binding template="ToastText01">
<text id="1">bodyText</text>
</binding>
</visual>
</toast>```
ToastText02	```<toast>
<visual>
<binding template="ToastText02">
<text id="1">headlineText</text>
<text id="2">bodyText</text>
</binding>
</visual>
</toast>```
ToastText03	```<toast>
<visual>
<binding template="ToastText03">
<text id="1">headlineText</text>
<text id="2">bodyText</text>
</binding>
</visual>
</toast>```
ToastText04	```<toast>
<visual>
<binding template="ToastText04">
<text id="1">headlineText</text>
<text id="2">bodyText1</text>
<text id="3">bodyText2</text>
</binding>
</visual>
</toast>```
ToastImageAndText01	```<toast>
<visual>
<binding template="ToastImageAndText01">
<image id="1" src="image1" alt="image1"/>
<text id="1">bodyText</text>
</binding>
</visual>
</toast>```

(continued)

Table 7-1. (*continued*)

Template name	XML snippet

ToastImageAndText02	```<toast>```
	 ``` <visual>```
	 ``` <binding template="ToastImageAndText02">```
	 ``` <image id="1" src="image1" alt="image1"/>```
	 ``` <text id="1">headlineText</text>```
	 ``` <text id="2">bodyText</text>```
	 ``` </binding>```
	 ``` </visual>```
	 ```</toast>```

ToastImageAndText03	```<toast>```
	 ``` <visual>```
	 ``` <binding template="ToastImageAndText03">```
	 ``` <image id="1" src="image1" alt="image1"/>```
	 ``` <text id="1">headlineText</text>```
	 ``` <text id="2">bodyText</text>```
	 ``` </binding>```
	 ``` </visual>```
	 ```</toast>```

ToastImageAndText04	```<toast>```
	 ``` <visual>```
	 ``` <binding template="ToastImageAndText04">```
	 ``` <image id="1" src="image1" alt="image1"/>```
	 ``` <text id="1">headlineText</text>```
	 ``` <text id="2">bodyText1</text>```
	 ``` <text id="3">bodyText2</text>```
	 ``` </binding>```
	 ``` </visual>```
	 ```</toast>```

Toasts with Images

Let's spice up that toast with some images. First, we'll create a second piece of XAML to put next to the one we already have using the code in Listing 7-4.

Listing 7-4. XAML Snippet for Toast with Images

```
<Button Content="Show toast with image" HorizontalAlignment="Left" VerticalAlignment="Top"
Margin="53,149,0,0" Click="ButtonSendNotificationWithImageClick" Grid.Column="1"/>
<TextBlock HorizontalAlignment="Left" Margin="13,15,0,0" TextWrapping="Wrap" Text="text / image
toast" VerticalAlignment="Top" Style="{StaticResource SubheaderTextStyle}" Width="308"
Grid.Column="1"/>
<TextBox x:Name="TextboxToastTextWithImage" HorizontalAlignment="Left" TextWrapping="Wrap"
VerticalAlignment="Top" Margin="10,93,0,0" Width="272" Grid.Column="1"/>
```

Pretty much the same template. Add an image to the Assets folder in the solution. I've chosen the new Microsoft logo for this demo. I'm using the ToastImageAndText01 template (see Table 7-1 for the XML structure).

On to the code we go! The code in Listing 7-5 is pretty much the same as that used for sending the text-only toast.

Listing 7-5. Toast with Image

```
private void ButtonSendNotificationWithImageClick(object sender, RoutedEventArgs e)
{
    var notifier = ToastNotificationManager.CreateToastNotifier();

var template = ToastNotificationManager.GetTemplateContent(ToastTemplateType.ToastImageAndText01);

    var element = template.GetElementsByTagName("text")[0];
    ((XmlElement)template.GetElementsByTagName("image")[0]).SetAttribute("src",
"ms-appx:///Assets/mslogo.png");

    element.AppendChild(template.CreateTextNode(TextboxToastTextWithImage.Text.Trim()));

    var toast = new ToastNotification(template);
    notifier.Show(toast);
}
```

The only difference here is that we need to find the image element and set the path to the image as a value. We can use both web images and local images. There is a restriction of 200KB for images. Remember, images included in the project can be referenced by using the ms-appx:/// structure. Spin up the app, type some text in the text box, and watch in awe as you see your image appear in a toast, as shown in Figure 7-4.

Figure 7-4. *Toast with an image*

Scheduling a Notification

So we have pretty toast messages now. Wouldn't it be nice if we could schedule one to appear when we want? Luckily for us, that kind of behavior is available out of the box. The only thing we need to do is create a ScheduledToastNotification instead of a ToastNotification and pass in the date and time we want the toast to pop up. First, we have to apply yet another XAML snippet, as shown in Listing 7-6.

Listing 7-6. XAML Snippet for scheduledToast UI

```
<Button Content="Schedule toast" HorizontalAlignment="Left" VerticalAlignment="Top"
Margin="53,149,0,0" Click="ButtonSendScheduledNotificationClick" Grid.Column="2"/>
<TextBlock HorizontalAlignment="Left" Margin="13,15,0,0" TextWrapping="Wrap" Text="scheduled toast"
VerticalAlignment="Top" Style="{StaticResource SubheaderTextStyle}" Width="308" Grid.Column="2"/>
<TextBox x:Name="TextboxTime" HorizontalAlignment="Left" TextWrapping="Wrap" VerticalAlignment="Top"
Margin="10,93,0,0" Width="272" Grid.Column="2"/>
```

What we're doing here is setting the value that's entered in the text box as the number of seconds to wait before the toast shows up. In a real-life situation, you would obviously check if the user entered a numeric value or even better use a numeric-only text box. The code behind the button looks, again, pretty familiar, as shown in Listing 7-7.

Listing 7-7. Schedule a Notification

```
private void ButtonSendScheduledNotificationClick(object sender, RoutedEventArgs e)
{
    var notifier = ToastNotificationManager.CreateToastNotifier();
    var template = ToastNotificationManager.GetTemplateContent(ToastTemplateType.
ToastImageAndText01);

    var element = template.GetElementsByTagName("text")[0];
    ((XmlElement)template.GetElementsByTagName("image")[0]).SetAttribute("src",
"ms-appx:///Assets/mslogo.png");

    element.AppendChild(template.CreateTextNode(string.Format("This toast appeared after {0}
seconds", TextboxTime.Text)));

    var date = DateTime.Now.AddSeconds(Convert.ToInt32(TextboxTime.Text));
    var scheduledToast = new ScheduledToastNotification(template, date);
    notifier.AddToSchedule(scheduledToast);
}
```

The first part of this code is exactly the same as in the previous examples. The difference is in the last lines where we take the current date and add the seconds entered in the text box. As mentioned earlier, we create a new ScheduledToastNotification instance instead of the, by now familiar, ToastNotification. The ScheduledToastNotification takes in the template and a DateTime stating when it needs to show up. The text will show the amount of seconds the toast waited, as shown in Figure 7-5.

Figure 7-5. A wild scheduled toast appears

An overload on the ScheduledToastNotification constructor enables a toast to pop up multiple times. Apply the code in Listing 7-8 to set the notification overload.

Listing 7-8. Notification Overload

```
var scheduledToast = new ScheduledToastNotification(template, date, new TimeSpan(0, 0, 1, 0), 2);
```

The first two parameters are the same as that in the first overload. The third one is a TimeSpan defining the interval time between pop-ups. This value has to be between 60 seconds and 60 minutes, anything else will show an error, as shown in Figure 7-6. The fourth parameter is the number of times the toast should show itself.

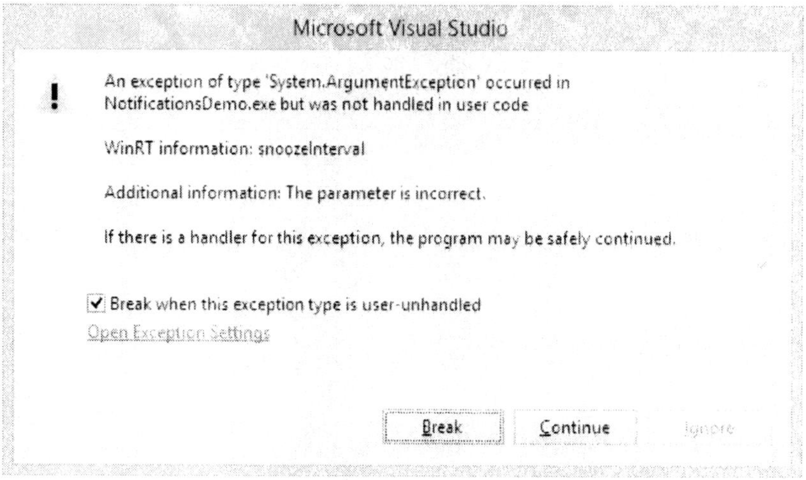

Figure 7-6. *Exception*

Adding Audio to Toasts

So far we've built normal text toasts, toasts with images, and toasts that show up at a certain time. Let's start creating some noise by adding audio notifications to toast messages. And let me immediately add that it's not possible to attach your own audio files to these notifications. So no heavy metal toasts, unfortunately. There are a bunch of available audio notifications, divided into looping and nonlooping notification. Table 7-2 lists them for you.

Table 7-2. *Notification Sounds*

Looping	Nonlooping
Notification.Looping.Alarm	Notification.Default
Notification.Looping.Alarm2	Notification.IM
Notification.Looping.Call	Notification.Mail
Notification.Looping.Call2	Notification.Reminder
	Notification.SMS

To use an audio notification, we need to create a new XML element in the template called "audio" and set its src attribute to one of the notifications in Table 7-2. I've added a new button to the text notification part for this. Listing 7-9 presents the code for that button.

Listing 7-9. Send Notification with Sound

```
private void ButtonSendNotificationWithSoundClick(object sender, RoutedEventArgs e)
{
    var notifier = ToastNotificationManager.CreateToastNotifier();
    var template = ToastNotificationManager.GetTemplateContent(ToastTemplateType.ToastText01);

    var element = template.GetElementsByTagName("text")[0];
    element.AppendChild(template.CreateTextNode(TextboxToastText.Text.Trim()));
```

```
XmlElement audioElement = template.CreateElement("audio");
audioElement.SetAttribute("src", "ms-winsoundevent:Notification.SMS");

var toast = new ToastNotification(template);
notifier.Show(toast);
}
```

Here you see that after appending the text box text to the template, we create the new element and set the src attribute to be Notification.SMS. When you want to play a looping notification, you also need to set the loop attribute to true:

```
audioElement.SetAttribute("loop", "true");
```

Go ahead and give it a try.

This was an overview of the most important toast notification features. In the next section we'll take a look at how to integrate your application with the Windows 8 lockscreen.

Lockscreen Notifications

A neat feature from Windows Phone has found its way into Windows 8 in an improved form. Those of you who have used Windows Phone will probably know the small icons on the lockscreen notifying you of missed calls, new text messages, and e-mails. Those lockscreen notifications are also available on Windows 8, and developers can leverage that functionality into their own applications.

Before we go figure this out in code, go to your Settings charm and choose Change PC settings. Somewhere in that Control panel you should find the settings shown in Figure 7-7.

Lock screen apps

Choose apps to run in the background and show quick status and notifications, even when your screen is locked

Choose an app to display detailed status

Figure 7-7. Lockscreen settings

Here we can see the big limitation on these notifications. Each Windows installation can have a maximum of seven apps showing notifications and only one showing a detailed notification on the lockscreen. In my case here, I still have two spots left, but as more and more apps become available on the store that allows this, it will fill up quickly. So when you decide to use the lockscreen functionality in your app, don't use it for anything that your app really depends on as you're just not sure that it will even show up at all.

With that in mind, let's get to work. Before we can write any code, we need to set some data into the manifest again, so double-click that, by now, very familiar file. On the Application UI tab, there should be an option called Badge Logo. Here we can set the type of lockscreen notification we want, either just a badge or badge and text (normal or detailed status, as shown in Figure 7-7). Set it to Badge, and you'll notice a bunch of scary looking red check marks, as shown in Figure 7-8.

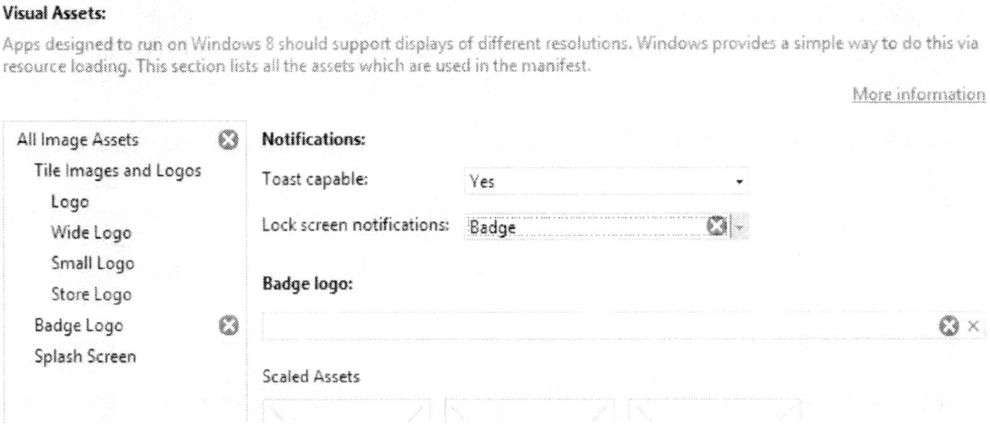

Visual Assets:

Apps designed to run on Windows 8 should support displays of different resolutions. Windows provides a simple way to do this via resource loading. This section lists all the assets which are used in the manifest.

More information

All Image Assets ⊗	**Notifications:**	
Tile Images and Logos	Toast capable:	Yes ▾
Logo		
Wide Logo	Lock screen notifications:	Badge ⊗ ▾
Small Logo		
Store Logo	**Badge logo:**	
Badge Logo ⊗		⊗ ×
Splash Screen		
	Scaled Assets	

Figure 7-8. *Lockscreen settings in manifest*

Figure 7-9 shows the reason for these check marks.

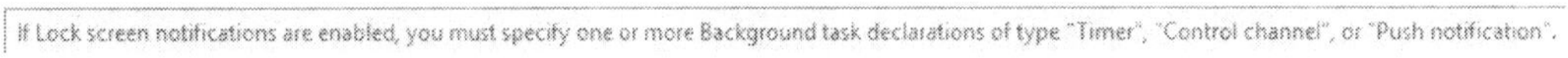

If Lock screen notifications are enabled, you must specify one or more Background task declarations of type "Timer", "Control channel", or "Push notification".

Figure 7-9. *Error description*

We need to specify a logo to display on the lockscreen. Specify anything you want as long as it's in one of those three resolutions. Microsoft advises you to select a monochrome image to have a better tie-in with the entire modern UI guidelines, so I would advise you to do the same. But rebel as I am, I'm going to use Microsoft's own, very colorful logo again to show on the lockscreen. After you select a logo, some red check marks will disappear, but not all of them. Those lockscreen notifications are greedy things, aren't they? Let's see what they're complaining about now. The same error description is shown for those still checked, as shown in Figure 7-9.

Apparently they want you to use background tasks to update your lockscreen. It's a pretty safe bet that those updates will occur when the app itself is not running, but for example purposes, we'll just define a background task but won't use it for now (this was discussed in depth in Chapter 6). In the manifest, go to the Declarations tab and select Background Tasks from the drop-down, then click the Add button. Background tasks need a task of type push, timer, or control channel. In this case, I've selected Timer just to have one. A background task also needs an entry point, in our case I've used the MainPage. Figure 7-10 shows these settings.

Properties:

Supported task types

☐ Audio

☐ Control channel

☐ System event

☑ Timer

☐ Push notification

App settings

Executable: _____

Entry point: NotificationsDemo.MainPage

Start page: _____

Figure 7-10. *Background task*

With all that in place, we can finally get some coding done. I've added another similar looking piece of XAML to the page, as shown in Listing 7-10. This time the number entered in the text box will be set as the number on the lockscreen.

Listing 7-10. XAML Snippet

```
<Button Content="set lockscreen" HorizontalAlignment="Left" VerticalAlignment="Top"
Margin="60,149,0,0" Click="ButtonSetLockScreenClick" Grid.Row="1"/>
<TextBlock HorizontalAlignment="Left" Margin="10,10,0,0" TextWrapping="Wrap" Text="lockscreen badge"
VerticalAlignment="Top" Style="{StaticResource SubheaderTextStyle}" Width="308" Grid.Row="1"/>
<TextBox x:Name="TextboxToastText_Copy" HorizontalAlignment="Left" TextWrapping="Wrap"
VerticalAlignment="Top" Margin="10,93,0,0" Width="272" Grid.Row="1"/>
```

And on to the code we go, as shown in Listing 7-11.

Listing 7-11. Setting the App to Lockscreen

```
private void ButtonSetLockScreenClick(object sender, RoutedEventArgs e)
{
    var lockscreen = BadgeUpdateManager.GetTemplateContent(BadgeTemplateType.BadgeNumber);
    var template = lockscreen.GetElementsByTagName("badge");
    ((XmlElement)template[0]).SetAttribute("value", TextboxLockScreen.Text);

    BadgeNotification badge = new BadgeNotification(lockscreen);
    BadgeUpdateManager.CreateBadgeUpdaterForApplication().Update(badge);
}
```

My, my, this does look mighty familiar! First, we get a template, either BadgeNumber or BadgeGlyph. Then we set the value attribute on the badge element. We won't get any errors when entering text instead of numbers in the text box, but there won't be any badge on the lockscreen. If there already was one, it will have now disappeared. Also, any number greater than 99 will just show up as 99+ on the lockscreen. Go ahead and try it out.

Since it's not possible to take a screenshot of the lockscreen, you'll just have to believe me that this code really does work. You can try it out and be amazed! If you are curious how they look, you can look at the figures in Chapter 6 about live tiles, the badges on the tiles look the same.

Summary

This chapter has discussed the use of notifications through toasts and lockscreen badges. With toasts, we can notify the user when a task completes or when some event occurs. Toasts can be created from within the app or from a background agent. We can use a wide range of templates, a lot like the way we used live tiles in the previous chapter. Toasts can include text, images, and even audio notifications. Although we can't add our own sounds, we can use the ones included in Windows 8.

Next to toasts, we can also use lockscreen notifications; however, there is a small catch when using those. The Windows 8 lockscreen can only hold up to seven notifications, and it's up to the user what those seven apps are. There is no way we can control that from within the app. So don't try to use lockscreen notifications to show really important data, it's just not built for that.

In the next chapter, we'll have a look at how to make your app behave properly on different form factors, resolutions, and states. I'm ready when you are!

CHAPTER 8

Building an Adaptable App

I have obtained many of my XAML skills through developing Windows Phone 7 applications. One of the biggest advantages for developers working on the Windows Phone 7 platform is the fact that Windows Phone 7 only has one resolution. Every application is built on a 480 × 800 resolution, and each and every device works only on that particular resolution. No need for us developers to keep different aspect ratios and resolutions in mind! Worst-case scenario, we implemented portrait and landscape modes, and even that is quite easy with the Visual State Manager (I'll discuss this later in the chapter).

When moving to Windows Phone 8 or Windows 8, I suddenly had to keep all these different devices, resolutions, and aspect ratios in mind, especially in Windows 8, where there are many supported resolutions. Luckily XAML makes it pretty easy to build an adaptable layout, and the Windows Store SDK team did a good job of giving us some controls that adjust their layout automatically depending on the amount of screen real estate they are given.

This chapter will look at how to implement different resolutions and test those different resolutions on one device. We'll also have a closer look at the Visual State Manager and how it helps us with implementing both portrait and landscape modes and with snapped applications.

Multiple Resolutions

Windows Store applications support a multitude of applications. The minimal resolution is 1024 × 768; if a device has a lower resolution, the app will give an error message stating that the app cannot open. A width of 1366 is needed in order to make applications snap to the side. When developing a Windows Store application, we can test different resolutions both in the Visual Studio designer as well as in the Windows simulator.

Grids

Open up Visual Studio 2012, start a new Windows Store project, and open the `MainPage.xaml` in design view. The XAML snippet in Listing 8-1 shows a grid that I've placed onto the `MainPage.xaml`, and it has its size and margins defined with absolute values.

Listing 8-1. Grid with Absolute Sizing

```
<Grid HorizontalAlignment="Left" Height="748" Margin="10,10,0,0" VerticalAlignment="Top"
Width="1346">
    <Grid.Background>
        <LinearGradientBrush EndPoint="0.5,1" StartPoint="0.5,0">
            <GradientStop Color="Black"/>
            <GradientStop Color="#FF0046FF" Offset="1"/>
            <GradientStop Color="Red"/>
```

```
            <GradientStop Color="#FF8BFF00" Offset="0.49"/>
        </LinearGradientBrush>
    </Grid.Background>
</Grid>
```

It is an ugly-looking grid with all those gradients in them, but the colors will help me prove my point. In the Visual Studio 2012 designer, the app should look like the one in Figure 8-1.

Figure 8-1. *The grid in design mode*

That looks great right? The grid seems to fill the entire screen. However, when I run the app, it looks like the one shown Figure 8-2.

Figure 8-2. *The app at runtime*

▬ **Note**   Depending on the resolution of your device, the result might differ from the screenshots in this chapter.

That doesn't look quite right. The reason is that the design mode in Visual Studio 2012 is set to a resolution of 1366 × 768, while my screen has a resolution of 1600 × 900, resulting in the black bars on the right and bottom of the grid. Let's fix this, adjust the grid as indicated in Listing 8-2.

Listing 8-2. Adaptable Grid

```
<Grid Margin="10">
    <Grid.Background>
        <LinearGradientBrush EndPoint="0.5,1" StartPoint="0.5,0">
            <GradientStop Color="Black"/>
            <GradientStop Color="#FF0046FF" Offset="1"/>
            <GradientStop Color="Red"/>
            <GradientStop Color="#FF8BFF00" Offset="0.49"/>
        </LinearGradientBrush>
    </Grid.Background>
</Grid>
```

Notice that the width and height properties are gone. When they are not set, the grid will fill up the entire available space that it gets from its parent. The margin of 10 makes sure that we leave a blank margin of 10 pixels on all sides of the grid. In the Visual Studio 2012 designer, nothing has changed, but when we run the application on any resolution, it looks like the one shown in Figure 8-3.

Figure 8-3. *The scaled app*

Now that we know how to build a page width control, let's try adding some scalable controls inside the grid.

The grid in Listing 8-3 shows a grid divided into rows and columns. Some cells contain a border control with a background color again to prove my point.

Listing 8-3. Grid with Borders

```
<Grid Background="{StaticResource ApplicationPageBackgroundThemeBrush}" Margin="0,0,0,10">
    <Grid.RowDefinitions>
        <RowDefinition Height="229"/>
        <RowDefinition Height="279"/>
        <RowDefinition Height="250"/>
    </Grid.RowDefinitions>
    <Grid.ColumnDefinitions>
        <ColumnDefinition Width="457"/>
        <ColumnDefinition Width="484"/>
        <ColumnDefinition Width="425"/>
    </Grid.ColumnDefinitions>
    <Border BorderBrush="Black" BorderThickness="1" Grid.Column="1" Background="#FFF30B0B"/>
    <Border BorderBrush="Black" BorderThickness="1" Grid.Row="1" Background="#FF095EF3"/>
    <Border BorderBrush="Black" BorderThickness="1" Grid.Column="1" Grid.Row="2"
    Background="#FF2DFB0D"/>
    <Border BorderBrush="Black" BorderThickness="1" Grid.Column="2" Grid.Row="1"
    Background="#FFE4EE15"/>

</Grid>
```

Figure 8-4 shows the resultant design in Visual Studio 2012.

Figure 8-4. Grid in design view

The grid doesn't have any width or height set, so it should scale to our resolution, right? Let's run the app and find out. Figure 8-5 shows the results.

Figure 8-5. Grid at runtime

That doesn't look right at all. Our grid did scale correctly, the problem this time lies in the row and ColumnDefinitions. They are set to absolute values, meaning they won't scale.

Change the grid as shown in Listing 8-4.

Listing 8-4. Grid with Scalable Rows and Columns

```
<Grid Background="{StaticResource ApplicationPageBackgroundThemeBrush}">
    <Grid.RowDefinitions>
        <RowDefinition Height="229*"/>
        <RowDefinition Height="279*"/>
        <RowDefinition Height="250*"/>
    </Grid.RowDefinitions>
    <Grid.ColumnDefinitions>
        <ColumnDefinition Width="457*"/>
        <ColumnDefinition Width="484*"/>
        <ColumnDefinition Width="425*"/>
    </Grid.ColumnDefinitions>
    <Border BorderBrush="Black" BorderThickness="1" Grid.Column="1" Background="#FFF30B0B"/>
    <Border BorderBrush="Black" BorderThickness="1" Grid.Row="1" Background="#FF095EF3"/>
    <Border BorderBrush="Black" BorderThickness="1" Grid.Column="1" Grid.Row="2"
    Background="#FF2DFB0D"/>
    <Border BorderBrush="Black" BorderThickness="1" Grid.Column="2" Grid.Row="1"
    Background="#FFE4EE15"/>

</Grid>
```

The only change here is that the height from the RowDefinitions and the width from the ColumnDefinitions now have a * behind their values. The XAML parser will take the ratio of the rows and columns and will apply those ratios to the actual size of the grid on the device. The results are shown in Figure 8-6.

Figure 8-6. *Scaled rows and columns in a grid*

Another option to define relative sizes is shown in Listing 8-5.

Listing 8-5. Another Way of Relative Sizing

```
<Grid Background="{StaticResource ApplicationPageBackgroundThemeBrush}">
    <Grid.RowDefinitions>
        <RowDefinition Height="Auto"/>
        <RowDefinition Height="*"/>
        <RowDefinition Height="*"/>
    </Grid.RowDefinitions>
    <Grid.ColumnDefinitions>
        <ColumnDefinition Width="457*"/>
        <ColumnDefinition Width="484*"/>
        <ColumnDefinition Width="425*"/>
    </Grid.ColumnDefinitions>
    <Border BorderBrush="Black" BorderThickness="1" Grid.Column="1" Height="100"
Background="#FFF30B0B"/>
    <Border BorderBrush="Black" BorderThickness="1" Grid.Row="1" Background="#FF095EF3"/>
    <Border BorderBrush="Black" BorderThickness="1" Grid.Column="1" Grid.Row="2"
Background="#FF2DFB0D"/>
    <Border BorderBrush="Black" BorderThickness="1" Grid.Column="2" Grid.Row="1"
Background="#FFE4EE15"/>

</Grid>
```

The first row is set to Auto, which means that the row height will scale depending on the controls inside that row. The Border in that row has a height of 100, so the first row will be 100 pixels high and the rest of the available space will be divided between the two remaining rows, as shown in Figure 8-7.

Figure 8-7. *Auto sizing the top row*

Testing Multiple Resolutions

To test our apps in different resolutions, we can use the simulator. On the side of the simulator sits a button that allows us to freely choose between seven different resolutions, as you can see in Figure 8-8. We've already discussed the simulator and its different options in Chapter 2.

Figure 8-8. *Resolutions in the simulator*

To switch to a different resolution, just select another resolution while the app is running in the simulator and it will resize on the fly.

The same trick applies when designing an application. When you are in design view in Visual Studio 2012, there is a view called Device. In that view we can switch resolutions and orientations. We can even snap the app in design view. Figure 8-9 shows the Device tab menu.

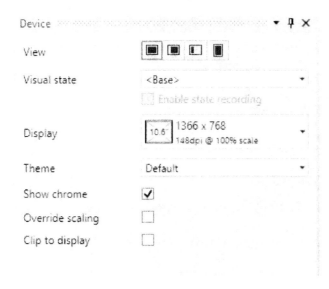

Figure 8-9. *Device view*

Figure 8-10 shows the available resolutions in the design view.

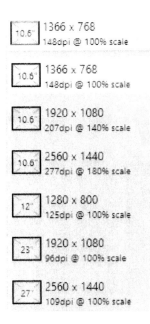

Figure 8-10. Resolutions in Visual Studio designer

Dots Per Inch

Resolution isn't the only thing that determines what an app looks like. Equally important is the DPI, also known as pixel density. Basically, it's the amount of pixels in a physical area. The higher your DPI is, the smaller your pixels are. A noticeable effect of DPI is on high-resolution screens, where the text seems to be very small. With Windows 8/RT we're seeing a big increase in devices with very high DPI values, like 11-inch tablets with full high-definition displays (1920 × 1080). Figures 8-11 and 8-12 show the same app on the same resolution (1920 × 1080). However, Figure 8-11 is a screenshot of the app running on a 10.6-inch screen with a DPI of 207, while Figure 8-12 is running on a 23-inch screen with a DPI of 96.

Figure 8-11. App on a 10.6-inch screen with a DPI of 207

Figure 8-12. *App on a 23-inch screen with a DPI of 96*

The difference between the two screenshots is most noticeable on the top row. Be sure to test your app not only on different resolutions but also on different DPI settings.

GridView

In addition to building controls in a scalable way, we need to scale the amount of items shown on the screen. The Windows 8 Start screen is one of the best examples here. Compare Figures 8-13 and 8-14, for example.

Figure 8-13. *Start screen at a higher resolution*

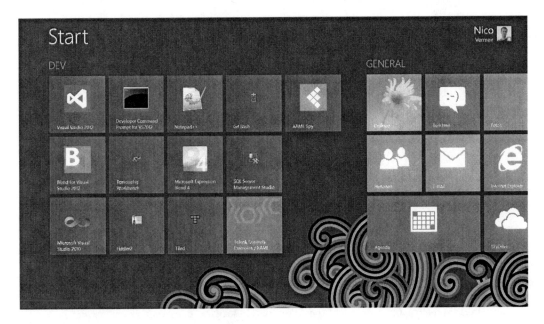

Figure 8-14. *Start screen at a smaller resolution*

See the difference? The first screenshot is from my laptop, taken at a resolution that is standard on this type of device. The second screenshot is taken at a resolution that is pretty common on netbooks and tablets. Windows 8 scales the Start screen so that all items fit on the screen vertically and makes it scroll horizontally. We get this kind of behavior out of the box when using a GridView. Listing 8-6 presents code for a GridView defined in XAML.

Listing 8-6. GridView in XAML

```
<GridView
x:Name="itemGridView"
AutomationProperties.AutomationId="ItemGridView"
AutomationProperties.Name="Grouped Items"
Grid.RowSpan="2"
Padding="116,137,40,46"
ItemsSource="{Binding Source={StaticResource groupedItemsViewSource}}"
ItemTemplate="{StaticResource Standard250x250ItemTemplate}"
SelectionMode="None"
IsSwipeEnabled="false"
IsItemClickEnabled="True"
ItemClick="ItemView_ItemClick">

<GridView.ItemsPanel>
    <ItemsPanelTemplate>
        <VirtualizingStackPanel Orientation="Horizontal"/>
    </ItemsPanelTemplate>
</GridView.ItemsPanel>
<GridView.GroupStyle>
```

```xml
<GroupStyle>
    <GroupStyle.HeaderTemplate>
        <DataTemplate>
            <Grid Margin="1,0,0,6">
                <Button
                    AutomationProperties.Name="Group Title"
                    Click="Header_Click"
                    Style="{StaticResource TextPrimaryButtonStyle}" >
                    <StackPanel Orientation="Horizontal">
                        <TextBlock Text="{Binding Title}" Margin="3,-7,10,10"
                        Style="{StaticResource GroupHeaderTextStyle}" />
                        <TextBlock Text="{StaticResource ChevronGlyph}" FontFamily="Segoe UI
                        Symbol" Margin="0,-7,0,10" Style="{StaticResource GroupHeaderTextStyle}"/>
                    </StackPanel>
                </Button>
            </Grid>
        </DataTemplate>
    </GroupStyle.HeaderTemplate>
    <GroupStyle.Panel>
        <ItemsPanelTemplate>
            <VariableSizedWrapGrid Orientation="Vertical" Margin="0,0,80,0"/>
        </ItemsPanelTemplate>
    </GroupStyle.Panel>
</GroupStyle>
</GridView.GroupStyle>
</GridView>
```

This actually is the GridView from the Grid App template included in the Windows Store SDK. For demo purposes, I've changed the height of the Standard250x250ItemTemplate to 150 in StandardStyles.xaml, as seen in Listing 8-7.

Listing 8-7. New Height in ItemTemplate

```xml
<DataTemplate x:Key="Standard250x250ItemTemplate">
    <Grid HorizontalAlignment="Left" Width="250" Height="150">
        <Border Background="{StaticResource ListViewItemPlaceholderBackgroundThemeBrush}">
            <Image Source="{Binding Image}" Stretch="UniformToFill" AutomationProperties.
            Name="{Binding Title}"/>
        </Border>
        <StackPanel VerticalAlignment="Bottom" Background="{StaticResource
        ListViewItemOverlayBackgroundThemeBrush}">
            <TextBlock Text="{Binding Title}" Foreground="{StaticResource
            ListViewItemOverlayForegroundThemeBrush}" Style="{StaticResource TitleTextStyle}"
            Height="60" Margin="15,0,15,0"/>
            <TextBlock Text="{Binding Subtitle}" Foreground="{StaticResource
            ListViewItemOverlaySecondaryForegroundThemeBrush}" Style="{StaticResource
            CaptionTextStyle}" TextWrapping="NoWrap" Margin="15,0,15,10"/>
        </StackPanel>
    </Grid>
</DataTemplate>
```

Figures 8-15 and 8-16 show the same app on the same resolutions as before.

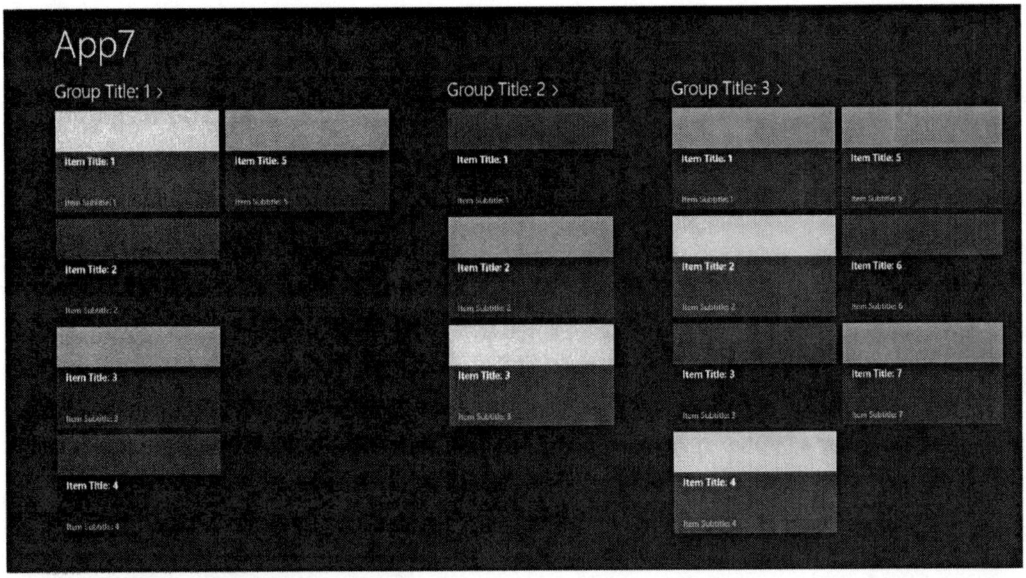

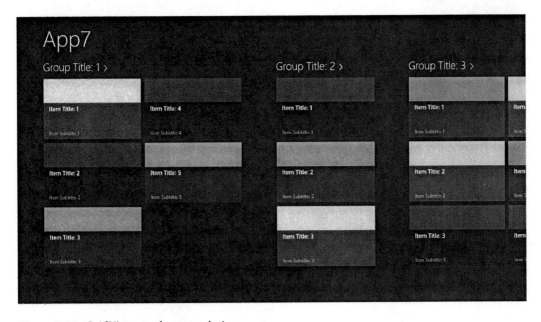

Figure 8-15. *GridView on a high resolution screen*

Figure 8-16. *GridView on a lower resolution screen*

This is default behavior, which makes the GridView a great control when displaying items. The SearchContract template uses this control to display the results.

Variable-Sized WrapGrid

Another great control introduced in Windows RT is the VariableSizedWrapGrid. This is a grid that can have some items stand out by making them span multiple rows and columns. Listing 8-8 shows an example.

Listing 8-8. VariableSizedWrapGrid

```
<VariableSizedWrapGrid MaximumRowsOrColumns="3" ItemHeight="44" ItemWidth="44">
    <Rectangle Fill="Red"/>
    <Rectangle Fill="Blue" Height="80"
            VariableSizedWrapGrid.RowSpan="2"/>
    <Rectangle Fill="Green" Width="80"
            VariableSizedWrapGrid.ColumnSpan="2"/>
    <Rectangle Fill="Yellow" Height="80" Width="80"
            VariableSizedWrapGrid.RowSpan="2"
            VariableSizedWrapGrid.ColumnSpan="2"/>
</VariableSizedWrapGrid>
```

As you can see, some elements are spanning multiple rows and columns, which results in something that looks like Figure 8-17.

Figure 8-17. *VariableSizedWrapGrid*

Changing the App Layout

We're now going to look at how we change the app layout by using the Visual State Manager to snap the app to the side and control the display under different device orientations.

Visual State Manager

The Visual State Manager (VSM) is a class that can change the appearance of XAML controls. It was introduced in Silverlight 2 and has found its way into the Windows RT framework. The VSM takes care of transitioning controls from one state into another. We can declare our own states or we can use the ones that are included in the templates.

The VSM contains VisualStateGroups, which is a collection of visual states. Those visual states can change the appearance of any control. The VSM is used throughout Windows Store applications for switching to snapped views or orientation changes. We can declare our own VisualStateGroups with some VisualStates as shown in Listing 8-9.

Listing 8-9. VisualStateGroup with VisualStates

```
<VisualStateGroup x:Name="DemoStateGroup">
    <VisualState x:Name="DemoState" />
    <VisualState x:Name="DemoStateWithStoryBoard">
        <Storyboard>
            <ObjectAnimationUsingKeyFrames Storyboard.TargetName="ItemsGridView"
            Storyboard.TargetProperty="Visibility">
                <DiscreteObjectKeyFrame KeyTime="0" Value="Collapsed" />
            </ObjectAnimationUsingKeyFrames>
        </Storyboard>
    </VisualState>
</VisualStateGroup>
```

First, we declare a `VisualStateGroup`, then we fill it with `VisualStates`. The first state is an empty one, and we might define this one in code. The second one has a storyboard that sets the Visibility property of the element with the name `ItemsGridView` to Collapsed. Listing 8-10 shows how we can switch VisualStates.

Listing 8-10. Switching VisualStates

```
VisualStateManager.GoToState(ItemsGridView, "DemoStateWithStoryBoard", false);
```

The first parameter is the control that we want to apply the state to, the second one is the name of the VisualState that we want to apply, and the third parameter determines if the Visual State Manager should try to execute a transition to that state.

Snap That App

As soon as a device has a horizontal resolution of 1366 pixels, apps can get snapped to the side. When snapped, an app takes up one-fourth of the available screen width. That means that our apps have less screen space, and we need to adjust our layout accordingly. Figure 8-18 shows the Grid App template in normal view, and Figure 8-19 shows the same app in snapped view.

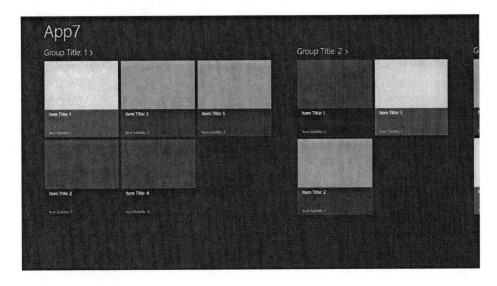

Figure 8-18. *Full view*

Figure 8-19. *Same app in snapped view*

The application shows the same information but uses a GridView in full-screen view and a ListView in snapped view. Listing 8-11 shows how the VSM takes care of changing the view.

Listing 8-11. VSM for Switching Between Full-Screen and Snapped Mode

```
<VisualState x:Name="FullScreenPortrait">
    <Storyboard>
        <ObjectAnimationUsingKeyFrames Storyboard.TargetName="backButton" Storyboard.
        TargetProperty="Style">
            <DiscreteObjectKeyFrame KeyTime="0" Value="{StaticResource PortraitBackButtonStyle}"/>
        </ObjectAnimationUsingKeyFrames>

        <ObjectAnimationUsingKeyFrames Storyboard.TargetName="itemGridView" Storyboard.
        TargetProperty="Padding">
            <DiscreteObjectKeyFrame KeyTime="0" Value="96,137,10,56"/>
        </ObjectAnimationUsingKeyFrames>
    </Storyboard>
</VisualState>

<VisualState x:Name="Snapped">
    <Storyboard>
        <ObjectAnimationUsingKeyFrames Storyboard.TargetName="backButton" Storyboard.
        TargetProperty="Style">
            <DiscreteObjectKeyFrame KeyTime="0" Value="{StaticResource SnappedBackButtonStyle}"/>
        </ObjectAnimationUsingKeyFrames>
        <ObjectAnimationUsingKeyFrames Storyboard.TargetName="pageTitle" Storyboard.
        TargetProperty="Style">
```

```
            <DiscreteObjectKeyFrame KeyTime="0" Value="{StaticResource
            SnappedPageHeaderTextStyle}"/>
        </ObjectAnimationUsingKeyFrames>

        <ObjectAnimationUsingKeyFrames Storyboard.TargetName="itemListView" Storyboard.
        TargetProperty="Visibility">
            <DiscreteObjectKeyFrame KeyTime="0" Value="Visible"/>
        </ObjectAnimationUsingKeyFrames>
        <ObjectAnimationUsingKeyFrames Storyboard.TargetName="itemGridView" Storyboard.
        TargetProperty="Visibility">
            <DiscreteObjectKeyFrame KeyTime="0" Value="Collapsed"/>
        </ObjectAnimationUsingKeyFrames>
    </Storyboard>
</VisualState>
```

We create two VisualStates: one for full-screen view and one for snapped view. In the VisualStates we have a storyboard that defines what happens with the controls on the page. When we switch to the Snapped VisualState, for example, we apply another style template to the Back button and the page title. After that we set the visibility for the GridView to Collapsed and the visibility for the ListView to Visible. The snapping of the app is handled by the operating system; all we need to do is make sure our app changes its appearance. The actual switching between the states is handled in the LayoutAwarePage.cs file, as shown in Listing 8-12.

Listing 8-12. Updating the VSM for Snapped View

```
public void StartLayoutUpdates(object sender, RoutedEventArgs e)
{
    var control = sender as Control;
    if (control == null) return;
    if (this._layoutAwareControls == null)
    {
        // Start listening to view state changes when there are controls interested in updates
        Window.Current.SizeChanged += this.WindowSizeChanged;
        this._layoutAwareControls = new List<Control>();
    }
    this._layoutAwareControls.Add(control);

    // Set the initial visual state of the control
    VisualStateManager.GoToState(control, DetermineVisualState(ApplicationView.Value), false);
}
```

The method calls DetermineVisualState to get the actual value for its current state. What DetermineVisualState does is obtains the value for the ApplicationViewState enumeration. That enumeration has four values: fullScreenLandscape, filled, snapped, or fullScreenPortrait. The page defines VisualStates for each of these values.

Building a useful snapped view for every page in your application is a big added value. The snapped views are a great idea with tons of possibilities. Each app should provide a decent, good-looking snapped view, unlike the Store app that's included in Windows 8. Its snapped view is shown in Figure 8-20.

Figure 8-20. *Windows Store snapped view*

Apps for social networks are great examples of useful snapped views. Having a live updating timeline snapped to the side while doing some work on the large part of the screen is a great feature (especially when you're as addicted to Twitter as I am). Another great example I have encountered is an app that functions as a remote for media center software. In full screen it shows information about the movie you're watching, when snapped it shows a remote with all the necessary controls.

Device Orientation

A series of devices with Windows 8 or Windows RT will have accelerometers. *Accelerometers* are sensors that detect device movement, and they are commonly used in games to control a character. Chapter 9 will explain how to implement the accelerometer in your own apps. The Windows operating system uses the accelerometer to detect if the user is holding the device in landscape or in portrait mode. This sensor is available on every tablet and on some laptops or ultrabooks. Since there is no way to specify that your app should only be made available on devices that don't have the accelerometer, we need to make sure that our apps can handle device rotation.

Like I've just explained, it's the LayOutAwarePage class that takes care of the rotation, so we literally have no extra work to provide this if we're including that class in our templates. However, it is up to us to make sure that our apps still look good. After all, our width becomes the height and vice versa. If you're using GridViews, you're good to go as this control scales automatically. If you're not using GridViews, follow the tips from the beginning of this chapter and be sure to test the app. If you don't have a device that can rotate, use the Windows simulator. It has buttons to rotate the view in every direction you want. Figure 8-21 shows a GridView in portrait mode.

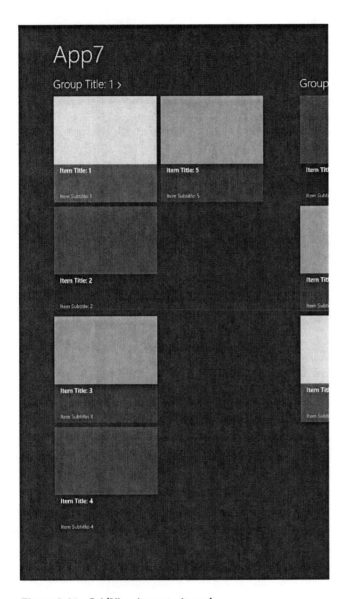

Figure 8-21. *GridView in portrait mode*

Summary

This chapter has taken a look at how to make sure our apps look good on any resolution. To do this, we've used relative sizes and GridViews. Relative values can scale according to the child control's sizes. They can also be set to take a certain percentage of the page instead of setting absolute values.

Next to making sure the app looks good on any resolution, we've also looked at implementing a snapped view by using the Visual State Manager. The VSM is a class that can change the appearance of any XAML control.

Last but not least, we've looked at how to test apps in portrait mode.

What I really want you to take away from this chapter is the importance of a layout that looks good in any resolution and that it's equally important to spend time building a decent snapped view. Make sure to test each and every page on all resolutions, snapped views, and orientations.

We also briefly discussed the accelerometer. The accelerometer is one of many sensors that can sit in a Windows 8 device. The next chapter will look at the most common sensors and how to implement them in our apps.

CHAPTER 9

Sensors

Sensors are a very important part of mobile applications, both on phones and tablets, and other form factors. They provide an alternative means of input or interaction with the device. There are a wide range of sensors in existence, and they provide a wide range of functions, from measuring the temperature to determining your location to knowing at what angle you're holding the device.

As developers, we have access to API functions that can read the sensor information. That way we can retrieve data relative to the user's position or build a game that is controlled by tilting the device and so forth. The possibilities are almost endless, especially when you start combining different sensors, for example, to build a racing game that is controlled by tilting the device but where the race track is actually the street you're currently standing on, effectively combining the location sensor and the accelerometer.

In this chapter we'll be discussing seven sensors:

- Accelerometer
- Location
- Simple orientation
- Light
- Inclinometer
- Gyroscope
- Compass

Many of these sensors have similar ways of reading their values, but we'll discuss them and what they actually do one by one. Let's get started!

Accelerometer Sensor

An accelerometer measures proper acceleration, or G force. The readings from an accelerometer could differ from what we would expect: an accelerometer in a device that is lying flat on a table, for example, would measure an upward acceleration due to its weight, while an accelerometer in free fall would measure nothing.

There are single axis and multiaxis accelerometers available: the single axis models only measure acceleration, while multiaxis models can also provide the angle at which they're moving. This is where Sony got the name for their PlayStation 3 controller Sixaxis. The controller contains an accelerometer with six axes, providing a pretty accurate motion control system.

How Does It Work?

An accelerometer contains a mass on a spring. When the device moves, the mass starts compressing the spring until it reaches the point where the mass moves at the same speed as the accelerometer. When that point is reached, the displacement of the mass is measured and that value is the readout of the sensor. Figure 9-1 shows how it works.

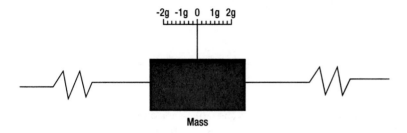

Figure 9-1. *Schematic representation of an accelerometer*

Using the Windows 8 Accelerometer API

Microsoft did a really great job in making the sensor APIs very easy to use. All we need to do is instantiate the `Windows.Devices.Sensors.Accelerometer` class and we're good to go. But first we'll need some UI, and Listing 9-1 provides the UI part for this first sensor.

Listing 9-1. UI for Accelerometer

```
<Grid Background="{StaticResource ApplicationPageBackgroundThemeBrush}">
    <Grid.RowDefinitions>
        <RowDefinition Height="*" />
        <RowDefinition Height="*" />
        <RowDefinition Height="*" />
    </Grid.RowDefinitions>
    <Grid.ColumnDefinitions>
        <ColumnDefinition Width="*" />
        <ColumnDefinition Width="*" />
        <ColumnDefinition Width="*" />
    </Grid.ColumnDefinitions>

    <StackPanel>
        <TextBlock Style="{StaticResource GroupHeaderTextStyle}" Text="Accelerometer" />
        <TextBox x:Name="AccelerometerValue" Margin="20" />
        <Button Margin="20"
                HorizontalAlignment="Left"
                VerticalAlignment="Top"
                Click="Button_Accelerometer"
                Content="Activate accelerometer" />
    </StackPanel>
</Grid>
```

We first define some three rows and three columns, splitting the app into a three-by-three grid. Every cell will contain the UI for a particular sensor. For the accelerometer, we have a text box that will contain the readout value and a button to start the sensor itself. Figure 9-2 shows the result.

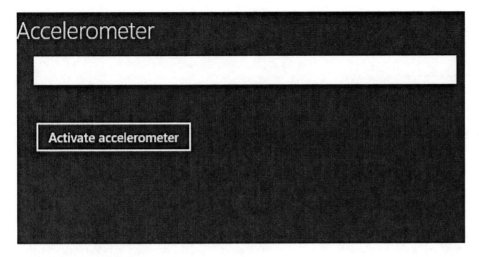

Figure 9-2. *UI for the accelerometer*

Now, for the code itself, as presented in Listing 9-2.

Listing 9-2. Instantiating the Accelerometer

```
private Accelerometer _accelerometer;
protected override void OnNavigatedTo(NavigationEventArgs e)
{
    _accelerometer = Accelerometer.GetDefault();
}
```

We first declare a field of type Accelerometer and then we call the GetDefault() method of that class. This returns the default instance of the accelerometer to us. Next, in Listing 9-3, we'll have a look at what the button does.

Listing 9-3. Accelerometer Button Event Handler

```
private async void Button_Accelerometer(object sender, RoutedEventArgs e)
{
    if (_accelerometer != null)
    {
        // Establish the report interval
        _accelerometer.ReportInterval = 10;

        //remove the handler first, In case it's already attached
        _accelerometer.ReadingChanged -= ReadingChanged;

        _accelerometer.ReadingChanged += ReadingChanged;
        _accelerometer.GetCurrentReading();
    }
}
```

```
        else
        {
            MessageDialog dialog = new MessageDialog("No accelerometer found");

            await dialog.ShowAsync();
        }
    }
}
```

The first thing we need to do when working with any sensor in Windows Store apps is check if the field has an instance. This is very important, because not every device contains every sensor. My daily developing machine, a normal everyday laptop without sensors or touchscreen, can only use the location sensor, all the other sensors are missing. Calling the GetDefault() method on a device that does not have the sensor you're trying to use will return null. So remember to check for an instance and provide some feedback to the user when the sensor is missing from the device, in this case we'll show a MessageDialog.

We first set the ReportInterval; this property determines how many milliseconds are between every readout of the sensor. It needs to be set to a value other than zero for the accelerometer to be able to work. Microsoft also states that when your app is no longer using the accelerometer to return the ReportInterval property to value zero, and this should provide for better battery life.

Once the ReportInterval is set, we attach a handler to the ReadingChanged event, and we get the current value of the sensor by calling GetCurrentReading();. Listing 9-4 shows the code for the ReadingChanged event handler.

Listing 9-4. ReadingChanged Event Handler

```
Private async void ReadingChanged(object sender, AccelerometerReadingChangedEventArgs e)
{
    await Dispatcher.RunAsync(CoreDispatcherPriority.Normal, () =>
    {
        AccelerometerReading reading = e.Reading;
        AccelerometerValue.Text = string.Format("X: {0}, Y: {1}, Z: {2}", reading.AccelerationX,
                                        reading.AccelerationY, reading.AccelerationZ);
    });
}
```

This method needs to be marked as async because we're using the Dispatcher to marshal this back to the UI thread. This Dispatcher task only takes care of showing the result in the text box, so it doesn't need any special priority, and we set it to CoreDispatcherPriority.Normal. The value that goes into the text box is a formatted string containing the X, Y, and Z axes values from the accelerometer.

Figure 9-3 shows what happens when the accelerometer is not available, and Figure 9-4 shows the result on a device with an accelerometer.

No accelerometer found

Close

Figure 9-3. *Device without an accelerometer*

Figure 9-4. *Accelerometer readouts*

Another useful event within the Accelerometer class is the Shaken event. This will fire when the user shakes the device. Having this method can really help developers because many apps will need to detect if the device is being shaken instead of requiring the precise coordinates of movement. The AccelerometerShakenEventArgs contains a TimeStamp property that will tell us when the Shaken event was fired. Listing 9-5 shows the code for a small example of the Shaken event.

Listing 9-5. Shaken Event

```
private async void Button_Accelerometer(object sender, RoutedEventArgs e)
{
    if (_accelerometer != null)
    {
        // Establish the report interval
        _accelerometer.ReportInterval = 10;

        //Window.Current.VisibilityChanged += new WindowVisibilityChangedEventHandler
        (VisibilityChanged);
        _accelerometer.ReadingChanged += new TypedEventHandler<Accelerometer,
        AccelerometerReadingChangedEventArgs>(ReadingChanged);

        _accelerometer.Shaken += AccelerometerOnShaken;
    }
    else
    {
        MessageDialog dialog = new MessageDialog("No accelerometer found");

        await dialog.ShowAsync();
    }

}
```

```
private void AccelerometerOnShaken(Accelerometer sender, AccelerometerShakenEventArgs args)
{
    var timeOfShake = args.Timestamp;
}
```

Location Sensor

The location sensor detects the current location of the device, either by using a GPS chip or by using triangulation. This is the only sensor that works on every device, as long as there's an active Internet connection. Figure 9-5 describes how triangulation works.

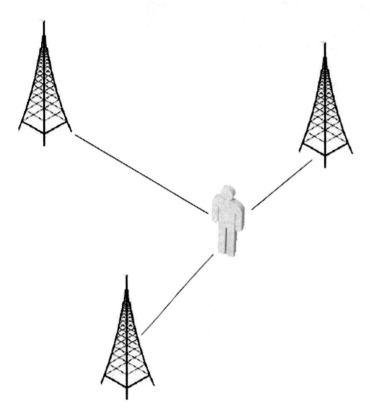

Figure 9-5. *Triangulation*

How Does It Work?

Location can come from a variety of sources. The best accuracy will come from an actual GPS chip, but other sources are Wi-Fi triangulation when using a registered public hotspot or your public IP address. Figure 9-6 shows how all these sources are abstracted into the Geolocator class.

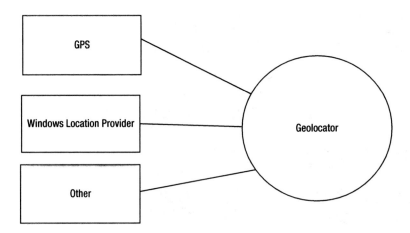

Figure 9-6. *Geolocator class*

As you can tell from this schematic, we as app developers don't have to worry where the location comes from. We just ask the Geolocator for a location and it will try all its sources to find one.

Using the Windows 8 Location API

Listing 9-6 shows the UI we'll be using for our location adventures.

Listing 9-6. UI for Location

```
<StackPanel Grid.Column="1">
    <TextBlock Style="{StaticResource GroupHeaderTextStyle}" Text="Location" />
    <TextBox x:Name="LocationValue" Margin="20" />
    <TextBox x:Name="LocationAddress" Margin="20" />
    <Button Margin="20"
            HorizontalAlignment="Left"
            VerticalAlignment="Top"
            Click="Button_Gps"
            Content="Activate Gps" />
</StackPanel>
```

There are two text boxes in this snippet: one will contain the latitude/longitude, while the other one will contain the actual address. Figure 9-7 shows the UI.

Figure 9-7. *Location UI*

Listing 9-7 shows how to instantiate and activate the Geolocator. This works a bit different from the other sensors.

Listing 9-7. Using the Geolocator

```
private Geolocator _geolocator;

private async void Button_Gps(object sender, RoutedEventArgs e)
{
    _geolocator = new Geolocator();

    _geolocator.PositionChanged += GeolocatorOnPositionChanged;

    await _geolocator.GetGeopositionAsync();
}
```

The Geolocator gets instantiated the old-fashioned way. We attach an event handler to the PositionChanged event and get the position. Listing 9-8 presents the code for the PositionChanged event handler.

Listing 9-8. PositionChanged Event Handler

```
private void GeolocatorOnPositionChanged(Geolocator sender, PositionChangedEventArgs args)
{
    Dispatcher.RunAsync(CoreDispatcherPriority.Normal, () =>
                    {
                        LocationValue.Text = string.Format("Lat: {0}, Lon: {1}",
                            args.Position.Coordinate.Latitude,
                            args.Position.Coordinate.Longitude);
                        LocationAddress.Text = string.Format("City: {0}, Country: {1}",
                            args.Position.CivicAddress.City, args.Position.CivicAddress.Country);
                    });
}
```

We once again use the Dispatcher to update UI, similar to the previous code with the accelerometer. The arguments have a Position property of type Geoposition. That type contains the Coordinate and the CivicAddress properties that we need here.

The Coordinate property also contains an Accuracy property, which shows precisely how the location is determined. With this information, we can make a guess at how the location was determined. Table 9-1 shows the accuracy and the likely used source. Figure 9-8 shows the result.

Table 9-1. *Accuracy to Source Relationship*

Accuracy	Likely source
1–10 meters	GPS with good position fix
10–100 meters	GPS with poor position fix
100–350 meters	Wi-Fi triangulation
Everything else	IP address

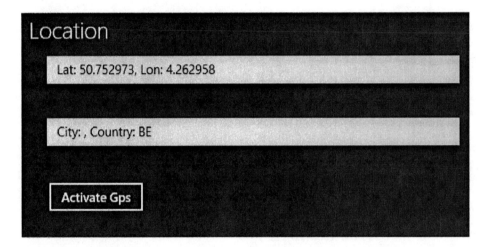

Figure 9-8. *Location result*

In this case the coordinates were determined by IP address, but they are quite close to my actual location, so use Table 9-1 with care as those values aren't written in stone.

Simple Orientation Sensor

The simple orientation sensor tells you in what quadrant the device is turned and if it's facing up or down. Figure 9-9 shows how the four quadrants of the device in the figure will register when rotated 90 degrees clockwise.

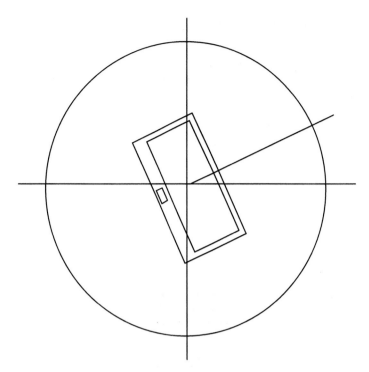

Figure 9-9. *How the simple orientation sensor registers rotation*

How Does It Work?

The simple orientation sensor is actually the same sensor as the orientation sensor; it's just an abstraction that takes the orientation sensor value and returns the quadrant the device is in.

Using the Windows 8 Simple Orientation API

Listing 9-9 shows the XAML code for this part of the app and Figure 9-10 shows how it looks.

Listing 9-9. XAML Snippet for the Simple Orientation UI

```
<StackPanel Grid.Column="2">
    <TextBlock Style="{StaticResource GroupHeaderTextStyle}" Text="Simple orientation" />
    <TextBox x:Name="SimpleOrientationValue" Margin="20" />
    <Button Margin="20"
            HorizontalAlignment="Left"
            VerticalAlignment="Top"
            Click="Button_SimpleOrientation"
            Content="Activate simple orientation sensor" />
</StackPanel>
```

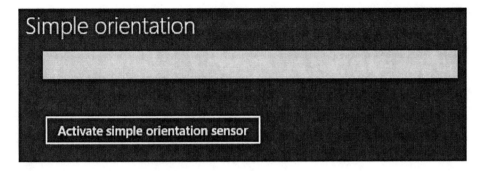

Figure 9-10. *The UI for simple orientation*

The SimpleOrientationSensor works very similar to the accelerometer, as seen in Listing 9-10.

Listing 9-10. Declaring and Getting the SimpleOrientationSensor

```
private SimpleOrientationSensor _simpleOrientationSensor;
protected override void OnNavigatedTo(NavigationEventArgs e)
{
    _simpleOrientationSensor = SimpleOrientationSensor.GetDefault();
}
```

No difference here; we declare a field and get the default SimpleOrientationSensor. If the returned value is null, then there's no sensor available in the current device. Listing 9-11 shows the code behind the button.

Listing 9-11. Simple Orientation Sensor Code

```
private async void Button_SimpleOrientation(object sender, RoutedEventArgs e)
{
    if (_simpleOrientationSensor == null)
    {
        MessageDialog dialog = new MessageDialog("No simple orientation sensor found");

        await dialog.ShowAsync();
    }
    else
    {
        _simpleOrientationSensor.OrientationChanged += SimpleOrientationSensorOnOrientationChanged;
        _simpleOrientationSensor.GetCurrentOrientation();
    }
}
```

As before, we check if the required sensor is found on our device; if it isn't, we show a warning, if it is, we handle the OrientationChanged event with the code in Listing 9-12.

Listing 9-12. OrientationChanged Event

```
private void SimpleOrientationSensorOnOrientationChanged(SimpleOrientationSensor sender,
SimpleOrientationSensorOrientationChangedEventArgs args)
{
    Dispatcher.RunAsync(CoreDispatcherPriority.Normal, () => DisplayOrientation
    (SimpleOrientationValue, args.Orientation));
}
```

Instead of setting the value here we call the DisplayOrientation method, passing in the text box and the detected orientation. The method is shown in Listing 9-13.

Listing 9-13. Method to Set a Text Depending on the Orientation in a Text Box

```
private void DisplayOrientation(TextBox tb, SimpleOrientation orientation)
{
    switch (orientation)
    {
        case SimpleOrientation.NotRotated:
            tb.Text = "Not Rotated";
            break;
        case SimpleOrientation.Rotated90DegreesCounterclockwise:
            tb.Text = "Rotated 90 Degrees Counterclockwise";
            break;
        case SimpleOrientation.Rotated180DegreesCounterclockwise:
            tb.Text = "Rotated 180 Degrees Counterclockwise";
            break;
        case SimpleOrientation.Rotated270DegreesCounterclockwise:
            tb.Text = "Rotated 270 Degrees Counterclockwise";
            break;
        case SimpleOrientation.Faceup:
            tb.Text = "Faceup";
            break;
        case SimpleOrientation.Facedown:
            tb.Text = "Facedown";
            break;
        default:
            tb.Text = "Unknown orientation";
            break;
    }
}
```

Pretty simple function! This takes the passed-in orientation and will set a text depending on the value of the orientation. Figure 9-11 shows the result.

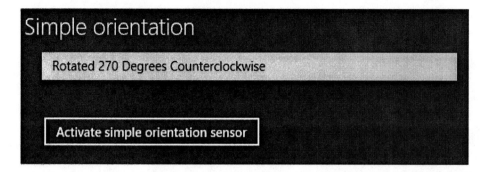

Figure 9-11. *Simple orientation sensor result*

Light Sensor

The light sensor detects the ambient light and returns a lux value, which is a measurement of the illuminance and how light the environment currently is, depending on the amount of ambient light detected.

How Does It Work?

Light sensors are diodes that are sensitive to certain wavelengths. Their response to a certain wavelength can be measured. The sensors found in most smartphones or tablets measure the levels of ambient light but cannot tell the difference in light color. Microsoft has published a nice table that shows the relation between lux values and lighting conditions. The table can be found on MSDN at
`http://msdn.microsoft.com/en-us/library/windows/desktop/dd319008(v=vs.85).aspx`.

Using the Windows 8 Light Sensor API

The light sensor is once again very similar to the accelerometer and the simple orientation sensors. Listing 9-14 shows the XAML for this part, and Listing 9-15 shows the field declaration.

Listing 9-14. UI Snippet for the Light Sensor

```
<StackPanel Grid.Row="1" Grid.Column="1">
    <TextBlock Style="{StaticResource GroupHeaderTextStyle}" Text="Light sensor" />
    <TextBox x:Name="LightSensorValue" Margin="20" />
    <Button Margin="20"
            HorizontalAlignment="Left"
            VerticalAlignment="Top"
            Click="Button_LightSensor"
            Content="Activate light sensor" />
</StackPanel>
```

Listing 9-15. Instantiating the Light Sensor

```
private LightSensor _lightSensor;
protected override void OnNavigatedTo(NavigationEventArgs e)
{
    _lightSensor = LightSensor.GetDefault();
}
```

Very similar, as I've mentioned before. Figure 9-12 shows what the UI looks like for this, and Listing 9-16 is the code for what happens when the button is clicked.

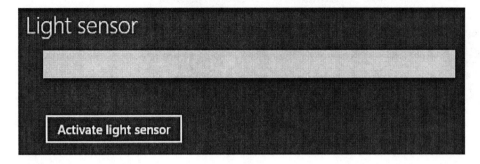

Figure 9-12. *Light sensor UI*

Listing 9-16. Code Behind the Button

```csharp
private async void Button_LightSensor(object sender, RoutedEventArgs e)
{
    if (_lightSensor == null)
    {
        MessageDialog dialog = new MessageDialog("No light sensor found");

        await dialog.ShowAsync();
    }
    else
    {
        _lightSensor.ReadingChanged += LightSensorOnReadingChanged;
        _lightSensor.GetCurrentReading();
    }
}
```

Again there is the null check to see if the sensor exists in the current device and an event handler attached to the ReadingChanged event. Listing 9-17 shows the code for that handler.

Listing 9-17. ReadingChanged Event Handler

```csharp
private async void LightSensorOnReadingChanged(LightSensor sender,
LightSensorReadingChangedEventArgs args)
{
    await Dispatcher.RunAsync(CoreDispatcherPriority.Normal, () =>
    {
        LightSensorReading reading = args.Reading;
        LightSensorValue.Text = String.Format("{0}", reading.IlluminanceInLux);
    });
}
```

The IlluminanceInLux property on the LightSensorReading class provides us with the amount of detected light expressed in lux. Figure 9-13 shows the result of a light sensor readout.

Figure 9-13. *Readout from Light sensor*

The next sensor that we'll look at is the inclinometer. (If you're thinking "The what now?" don't worry, that was my first reaction as well!)

Inclinometer Sensor

The inclinometer is also, and better, known as the tiltmeter. It measures angles of slope, elevation, and depression of an object with respect to gravity. The values it returns are pitch, yaw, and roll. These values can best be explained with an image, as shown in Figure 9-14.

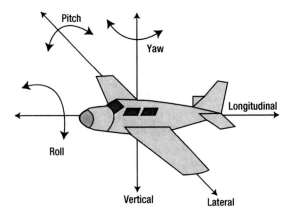

Figure 9-14. *Pitch, yaw, and roll*

How Does It Work?

An inclinometer generates an artificial horizon and measures the amount of tilt in respect to that horizon. Figure 9-15 illustrates the horizon and tilt.

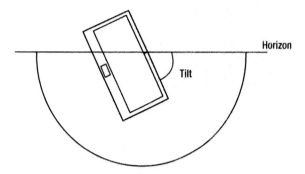

Figure 9-15. *Horizon and tilt*

Using the Windows 8 Inclinometer API

As usual, we'll begin with a piece of XAML. Listing 9-18 shows the UI for the inclinometer.

Listing 9-18. UI for Inclinometer

```
<StackPanel Grid.Row="1" Grid.Column="2">
    <TextBlock Style="{StaticResource GroupHeaderTextStyle}" Text="Inclinometer" />
    <TextBox x:Name="InclinoMeterValue" Margin="20" />
    <Button Margin="20"
            HorizontalAlignment="Left"
            VerticalAlignment="Top"
            Click="Button_Inclinometer"
            Content="Activate inclinometer" />
</StackPanel>
```

Same as before, a text box will show the value of the sensor, and there is a button to activate it. Figure 9-16 shows how it will look.

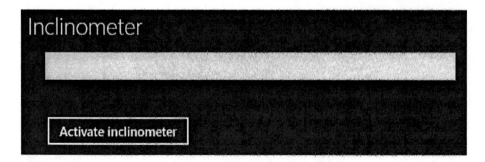

Figure 9-16. *UI for inclinometer*

In Listing 9-19, we'll see how to get the sensor instance, and the code for the button is shown in Listing 9-20.

Listing 9-19. Getting the Inclinometer Instance

```
private Inclinometer _inclinometer;
protected override void OnNavigatedTo(NavigationEventArgs e)
{
    _inclinometer = Inclinometer.GetDefault();
}
```

Listing 9-20. Activating the Sensor

```
private async void Button_Inclinometer(object sender, RoutedEventArgs e)
{
    if (_inclinometer == null)
    {
        MessageDialog dialog = new MessageDialog("No inclinometer found");

        await dialog.ShowAsync();
    }
    else
    {
        _inclinometer.ReadingChanged += InclinometerOnReadingChanged;
        _inclinometer.GetCurrentReading();
    }
}
```

So far nothing new. We check if the sensor has a value to make sure that the device has this type of sensor on board. And we start listening to the ReadingChanged event. Listing 9-21 shows the event handler.

Listing 9-21. ReadingChanged Event Handler

```
private async void InclinometerOnReadingChanged(Inclinometer sender,
InclinometerReadingChangedEventArgs args)
{
    await Dispatcher.RunAsync(CoreDispatcherPriority.Normal, () =>
    {
        InclinometerReading reading = args.Reading;
        InclinoMeterValue.Text = string.Format("Yaw: {0}, Pitch: {1}, Roll: {2}",
                                                reading.YawDegrees, reading.PitchDegrees,
                                                reading.RollDegrees);

    });
}
```

From the result we get yaw, pitch, and roll measured in degrees. Figure 9-17 shows the result.

Figure 9-17. *Inclinometer result*

Only two more sensors to go in this chapter. Let's have a look at the gyroscope and finish off with the compass.

Gyroscope Sensor

A gyroscope is a device that can measure rotation and orientation.

How Does It Work?

A mechanical gyroscope is a spinning disk in which the axle can assume any orientation. The disk itself rotates differently from the device, and the difference in that movement is measured. The electronic versions of this principle are called microelectromechanical system (MEMS) gyroscopes. These MEMS gyroscopes put the concept of the mechanical gyroscope in an electrical implementation. These are the types of gyroscopes usually found in smartphones, tablets, and other devices.

Using the Windows 8 Gyroscope API

Most of the code for the gyroscope is the same as with previous sensors. Listing 9-22 shows the XAML and Listing 9-23 show all the code at once.

Listing 9-22. UI Part for Gyroscope Function

```
<StackPanel Grid.Row="2" Grid.Column="0">
    <TextBlock Style="{StaticResource GroupHeaderTextStyle}" Text="Gyroscope" />
    <TextBox x:Name="GyroscopeValue" Margin="20" />
    <Button Margin="20"
            HorizontalAlignment="Left"
            VerticalAlignment="Top"
            Click="Button_Gyroscope"
            Content="Activate gyroscope" />
</StackPanel>
```

Listing 9-23. Declaring the Gyroscope, Activating It, and Responding to the Event

```
private Gyrometer _gyrometer;
protected override void OnNavigatedTo(NavigationEventArgs e)
{
    _gyrometer = Gyrometer.GetDefault();
}

private async void Button_Gyroscope(object sender, RoutedEventArgs e)
{
    if (_gyrometer == null)
    {
        MessageDialog dialog = new MessageDialog("No gyroscope found");

        await dialog.ShowAsync();
    }
    else
    {
        _gyrometer.ReadingChanged += GyrometerOnReadingChanged;
        _gyrometer.GetCurrentReading();
    }
}

private async void GyrometerOnReadingChanged(Gyrometer sender, GyrometerReadingChangedEventArgs args)
{
    await Dispatcher.RunAsync(CoreDispatcherPriority.Normal, () =>
    {
        GyrometerReading reading = args.Reading;
        GyroscopeValue.Text = string.Format("X: {0}, Y: {1}, Z:{2}", reading.AngularVelocityX,
        reading.AngularVelocityY, reading.AngularVelocityZ);
    });
}
```

The GyrometerReading provides us with angular velocity, measured in degrees per seconds on the X, Y, and Z axes. Figure 9-18 shows the result.

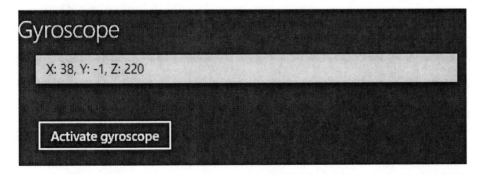

Figure 9-18. *Gyroscope result*

And last but not least, we'll have a look at how the compass works in Windows Store apps.

Compass Sensor

A compass is a device that can give a sense of direction relative to the surface of the earth by using the four cardinal directions (north, east, south, west).

How Does It Work?

The first compass worked with a needle that pointed to the magnetic north. Obviously there is no such thing inside our devices. What we have is called a magnetometer (this cannot be used to track the mutant villain Magneto by the way) or a solid state compass. A magnetometer comprises a number of magnetic field sensors that output a signal proportional to the device's direction.

Using the Windows 8 Compass API

Listing 9-24 shows the XAML and Listing 9-25 shows the code for the compass.

Listing 9-24. XAML for Compass UI

```
<StackPanel Grid.Row="2" Grid.Column="1">
    <TextBlock Style="{StaticResource GroupHeaderTextStyle}" Text="Compass" />
    <TextBox x:Name="CompassValue" Margin="20" />
    <Button Margin="20"
            HorizontalAlignment="Left"
            VerticalAlignment="Top"
            Click="Button_Compass"
            Content="Activate compass" />
</StackPanel>
```

Listing 9-25. Code for Compass

```
private Compass _compass;
protected override void OnNavigatedTo(NavigationEventArgs e)
{
    _compass = Compass.GetDefault();
}

private async void Button_Compass(object sender, RoutedEventArgs e)
{
    if (_compass == null)
    {
        MessageDialog dialog = new MessageDialog("No compass found");

        await dialog.ShowAsync();
    }
    else
    {
        _compass.ReadingChanged += CompassOnReadingChanged;
        _compass.GetCurrentReading();
    }
}
```

```
private async void CompassOnReadingChanged(Compass sender, CompassReadingChangedEventArgs args)
{
    await Dispatcher.RunAsync(CoreDispatcherPriority.Normal, () =>
    {
        CompassReading reading = args.Reading;
        CompassValue.Text = String.Format("{0}", reading.HeadingMagneticNorth);
        //CompassValue.Text = String.Format("{0}", reading.HeadingTrueNorth);
    });
}
```

The code is identical to that for the previous sensors, but the CompassReading provides a readout for magnetic north and true north. Aren't they the same? Apparently not. True north points to the north pole, while the magnetic north moves over time. It's the place where the earth's magnetic field is pointed vertically down. In 2012 the magnetic north was situated somewhere over Canada, and it moves at a speed of about 35 miles per year.

Figure 9-19 shows the result of the magnetic north readout. The value in Figure 9-19 shows the degrees the device is currently rotated away from the magnetic north.

Figure 9-19. *Compass readout*

Summary

In this chapter we've discussed the seven most widely used sensors that are available to us through the Windows RT APIs. The sensors we've discussed are:

- Accelerometer
- Location
- Simple orientation
- Light
- Inclinometer
- Gyroscope
- Compass

These sensors provide a wide range of information, ranging from where the device is to how it's being held or how much ambient light there is, a lot of information at our fingertips to get creative with!

Talking about creative, in the next chapter we'll briefly explore game development for the Windows Store. Always wanted to be a game developer? It's easier than you think (to get started at least).

■ ■ ■

CHAPTER 10

Games

Everyone who has ever played videogames has at least once dreamed of creating their very own game. I know I have, on more than one occasion. But games were built in C++ or some other low-level language, and, as a high-level developer, I am only familiar with languages like C# or Java. In 2004, Microsoft announced the XNA Framework, a framework that would make game development a breeze by allowing developers to use the power and simplicity of the .NET framework to build their games. But the framework didn't stop there. XNA allowed hobby game developers to launch their games on the popular Xbox 360 console, followed by Windows Phone 7 a few years later. Developers can now target three popular gaming platforms. In fact, every game available on Windows Phone 7 is built with XNA because the platform doesn't support anything else.

Fast forward to today, where XNA is very popular and widely used. But then Microsoft decides that Windows 8 doesn't get any support for the framework. Windows 8 games can only be built in JavaScript or C++. And the same goes for Windows Phone 8, although on the Windows Phone platform we can still use XNA because of backward compatibility with Windows Phone 7, but the new features like in-app purchases are not available. Needless to say, the XNA community was a bit disappointed with this news.

Direct3D

So what can we do today to build games for the Windows Store? There are two templates included in the Windows 8 SDK that can be found under the C++ language in the New Project screen—Direct2D and Direct3D—as shown in Figure 10-1.

Figure 10-1. *Direct2D and Direct3D templates*

The Direct3D template creates a project that when it is run shows a spinning cube like the one shown in Figure 10-2.

Figure 10-2. *The spinning cube of Direct3D*

I understand a bit of C++, but I can't write it myself. The code that is included in the template is pretty large, and since this book focuses on C#, I'm not even going to try to explain everything that is going on there. I will show you the project structure, and for that I direct you to Figure 10-3.

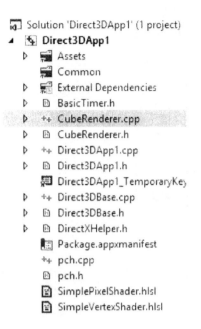

Figure 10-3. *Direct3D template project structure*

Quite a lot of code for just a template, but nothing we should worry about right now. Let's have a quick look at the Direct2D template.

Direct2D

The Direct2D template is an app that shows some text on a blue background. The app has an AppBar that, just like any Windows Store app, can be called by right-clicking or by dragging in from the top or bottom of the screen. There are two buttons on the AppBar that will switch between a number of background colors, as shown in Figure 10-4.

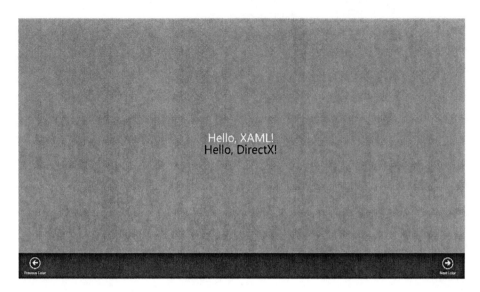

Figure 10-4. *Direct2D template*

The interesting thing about this template is that it contains an XAML page. It's starting to get a bit familiar here! It's still uses C++ for any logic, but the page itself is XAML. Listing 10-1 shows the XAML code of the page.

Listing 10-1. DirectXPage

```
<Page
    x:Class="Direct2DApp1.DirectXPage"
    xmlns="http://schemas.microsoft.com/winfx/2006/xaml/presentation"
    xmlns:x="http://schemas.microsoft.com/winfx/2006/xaml"
    xmlns:local="using:Direct2DApp1"
    xmlns:d="http://schemas.microsoft.com/expression/blend/2008"
    xmlns:mc="http://schemas.openxmlformats.org/markup-compatibility/2006"
    mc:Ignorable="d">
    <SwapChainBackgroundPanel x:Name="SwapChainPanel" PointerMoved="OnPointerMoved" PointerReleased=
"OnPointerReleased">
        <TextBlock x:Name="SimpleTextBlock" HorizontalAlignment="Center" FontSize="42" Height="72"
Text="Hello, XAML!" Margin="0,0,0,50"/>
    </SwapChainBackgroundPanel>
    <Page.BottomAppBar>
        <AppBar Padding="10,0,10,0">
            <Grid>
                <StackPanel Orientation="Horizontal" HorizontalAlignment="Left">
                    <Button Style="{StaticResource AppBarButtonStyle}"
                            Tag="Previous"
                            AutomationProperties.AutomationId="PreviousAppBarButton" Content="="&#xE112;"
                            AutomationProperties.Name="Previous Color"
                            Click="OnPreviousColorPressed"/>
                </StackPanel>
                <StackPanel Orientation="Horizontal" HorizontalAlignment="Right">
                    <Button Style="{StaticResource AppBarButtonStyle}"
                            Tag="Next"
```

```
                              AutomationProperties.AutomationId="NextAppBarButton" Content="="&#xE111;"
                              AutomationProperties.Name="Next Color"
                              Click="OnNextColorPressed"/>
                    </StackPanel>
                </Grid>
            </AppBar>
        </Page.BottomAppBar>
</Page>
```

Would you look at that? It really is the good old AppBar that we've been using throughout the book. The interesting part of this XAML tree, however, is the SwapChainBackgroundPanel. The SwapChainBackgroundPanel is a control that is used for DirectX interoperability, meaning it's just an XAML control but it can show DirectX rendering on a page. The control does have some limitations, such as it has to be the root element on a page and it cannot have any parents. Also, only one SwapChainBackgroundPanel can be on a page. And last but not least, the SwapChainBackgroundPanel inherits from the UIElement but not from Control, meaning it does not behave like a "normal" XAML control. You can't force it to get focus, for example.

You are probably wondering what use such a control could have. Let's compare it with XNA for a minute. In XNA (that is basically just a managed wrapper around DirectX), if we want some menus or heads-up display (HUD) controls on screen we need to render them ourselves, giving them a certain graphic and writing all the boiler plate code for handling clicks. In a game built with the Direct2D template, we can use normal XAML controls for the menus, and they will appear on top of the rendered image in the SwapChainBackgroundPanel. If I would add a button to the XAML of the Direct2D template, like in Listing 10-2, we would get the result shown in Figure 10-5.

Listing 10-2. Adding a Button to the SwapChainBackgroundPanel

```
<SwapChainBackgroundPanel x:Name="SwapChainPanel" PointerMoved="OnPointerMoved"
PointerReleased="OnPointerReleased">
    <TextBlock x:Name="SimpleTextBlock" HorizontalAlignment="Center" FontSize="42" Height="72"
Text="Hello, XAML!" Margin="0,0,0,50"/>
    <Button Margin="100, 20, 0, 0">Hello world from XAML!</Button>
</SwapChainBackgroundPanel>
```

Figure 10-5. *The button on top of the SwapChainBackgroundPanel*

The background color and the black text are being rendered by DirectX, while the buttons and the white text are being rendered by the XAML engine. Add a nice style to the XAML button and we could have a main menu up and running in no time, but it's still C++ code.

SharpDX

Where would we be without community? Whenever a software company like Microsoft launches a new software product, there will be communities that build something to make our lives easier or just more fun. A community project that I've had my eyes on since the launch of Windows 8 is SharpDX. Here's what the SharpDX site (http://www.sharpdx.org/) says about the project.

> *SharpDX is an open-source project delivering the full DirectX API under the .Net platform, allowing the development of high performance game, 2D and 3D graphics rendering as well as realtime sound application.*
>
> *SharpDX is built with a custom tool called SharpGen able to generate automatically a .NET API directly from the DirectX SDK headers, thus allowing a tight mapping with the native API while taking advantages of the great strength of the .Net ecosystem.*
>
> *SharpDX is fully supporting all Windows platforms including latest Windows 8 Metro and Windows Phone 8. Easily develop multimedia applications for desktop, WinRT and Windows Phone with the same API!*

When I first read this I immediately thought Sweet! They're rebuilding XNA! Turns out that that's not exactly what they are doing. The concept is quite similar, they are building a managed wrapper around DirectX, but it's still quite complicated to use. Should you want to try it you can either download a complete setup package, build it from source, or reference it using NuGet. The real interesting part of SharpDX is the projects that are built with it, one in particular called MonoGame, which is something we'll discuss in more detail.

MonoGame

So what's so special about MonoGame? MonoGame is an open source implementation of the XNA 4 framework. They have taken every single XNA 4 namespace and class and made their own implementation. They say that they didn't want to decompile the actual XNA binaries to prevent any lawsuits, so instead of copying they started to reinvent. MonoGame is currently on version 3 and has all major XNA 4 features on board, the latest addition being full 3D support. Games built on MonoGame currently work on iOS, Android, Linux, Mac OS X, Windows, Windows Phone 8, Windows Store, and PlayStation Mobile. That's a lot of platforms with the same code base (depending on the targeted platforms, some small code changes may be required). Xbox 360 and Windows Phone 7 are not supported but they support XNA, so the code should be interchangeable.

So how compatible is MonoGame code with XNA code actually? Well the (very) small game that we'll be building in this chapter is actually a demo that I've used in an XNA for a Windows Phone 7 101 session back when Windows Phone 7 was still new. I copied over the code from the Visual Studio 2010 solution to a new MonoGame project in Visual Studio 2012, replaced the touchscreen code by mouse code, and it was done. The drawing of art, the logic, everything worked just as well in MonoGame as it did in XNA. Figure 10-6 shows the game in its finished state. It's a Space Invaders-style game where the green square is the player that is moved with the mouse, and the left mouse button fires a laser. The blue squares at the top are the enemies.

Figure 10-6. *The game for this chapter*

I know it's not much to look at, but developing a great looking game would be a book all in itself, so we'll just cover the basics of MonoGame here. Should you get stuck anywhere while building a MonoGame game, you can search the MonoGame forums on their Codeplex web site (`http://monogame.codeplex.com/`) or just search the XNA forums. In my experience, about 95 percent of all XNA code just simply works in MonoGame. Before we start building, we'll need to install MonoGame first.

Installing MonoGame

To get started we'll need the MonoGame installer from the Codeplex site. We'll also need either the Windows Phone 8 SDK or Visual Studio 2010 (Express edition will do fine if you don't have access to a paid version). Why do we need this? Content files like images or sounds are formats that MonoGame doesn't understand. This is where the ContentPipeLine comes in. The ContentPipeLine is a separate project type that takes these content files and builds them into XNB files. The way it does this is by using ContentProcessors. MonoGame, just like XNA, has some ContentProcessors for the most common file types like MP3, WAV, JPG, PNG, and so on. Most standard image, sound, and font types are supported out of the box. Unsupported file types can be supported by writing your own ContentProcessor. But that's out of the scope for this book. Just remember that it is possible, and the implementation depends on the file type. Back to the original problem. ContentPipeLines generate XNB files that are supported by MonoGame. MonoGame doesn't have the ContentPipeLine project, so that's why we need either Visual Studio 2010 (to use a ContentPipeLine from XNA 4.0) or the Windows Phone 8 SDK (which brings XNA 4 support to Visual Studio 2012). When that prerequisite is installed, launch the installer to install MonoGame, Visual Studio Templates, dependencies, and so on. When that's finished, it's time to start building a game.

Starting a MonoGame Project

MonoGame installs some Visual Studio 2012 templates for us to use, as shown in Figure 10-7.

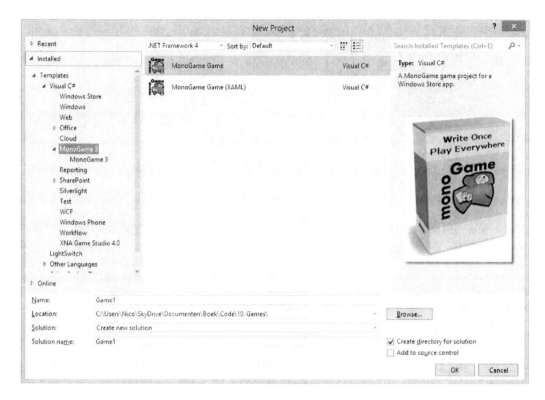

Figure 10-7. *MonoGame templates*

And just as you might expect, the MonoGame Game (XAML) template uses a `SwapChainBackgroundPanel`, just like the Direct2D template we discussed earlier. So we can build our entire menu structure using XAML. However, I would advise against using XAML for in-game controls. Using the XAML engine while rendering and playing your game will have a large performance impact, especially on lower-end machines like Windows RT devices. And I do speak from personal experience here; a game I'm working on works flawlessly on my developer machine but has terrible performance when launched on a Surface RT. So be careful there and make sure to test your games (or any app actually) on low-power devices.

When using XAML for your menu structure, there is no way to navigate between different pages since the root element is not a frame but a `SwapChainBackgroundPanel`. The only way to play around with menus is to place them in a container like a Grid or a StackPanel and swap the visibility of those containers as needed. Go ahead and create a new MonoGame game. Figure 10-8 shows the project structure.

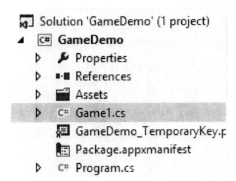

Figure 10-8. *MonoGame project structure*

Everything happens in the Game1.cs file. That's the main entry point of the game.

Try building the project, and you'll notice that there are some build errors, as shown in Figure 10-9.

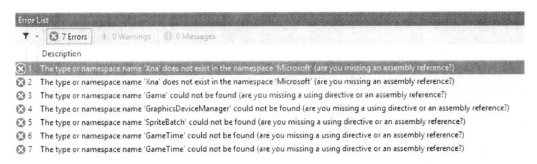

Figure 10-9. *Build errors*

That's because the template doesn't automatically reference the MonoGame framework. We can either add a reference to the DLL that sits inside the installation folder of MonoGame or we can add the MonoGame project with all sources to our solution. Here I've chosen the latter, as shown in Figure 10-10.

Figure 10-10. *MonoGame project added*

Don't forget to add a reference to the newly added project and try to build it again. It should work now. Let's have a look at the Game class next.

Game Class

Game1.cs already contains some fields and methods that we can use. We'll go over them from top to bottom. The first thing we encounter is the code in Listing 10-3.

Listing 10-3. Fields in Game1.cs

```
GraphicsDeviceManager _graphics;
SpriteBatch _spriteBatch;
```

The GraphicsDeviceManager handles everything that has to do with the graphics device inside your system. Things like setting the resolution and supported orientations are handled in this class. The SpriteBatch is something that we'll need when we start drawing stuff on our screen. It handles everything that has to do with drawing, both text and sprites (a sprite is a 2D image that we draw on screen, such as a player, a tree, or an enemy).

The constructor is where we initialize the GraphicsDeviceManager and where we tell the system the location of our content directory. The content directory is where it will search for the XNB files, as shown in Listing 10-4.

Listing 10-4. Game Constructor

```
public Game1()
{
    _graphics = new GraphicsDeviceManager(this);
    Content.RootDirectory = "Content";
}
```

Looks like we'll need a folder called Content. Add one to the project now and just leave it be for now. Moving on we reach the first method called Initialize(), as shown in Listing 10-5.

Listing 10-5. Initialize Method

```
protected override void Initialize()
{
    // TODO: Add your initialization logic here

    base.Initialize();
}
```

MonoGame is kind enough to tell us that this is the place for initialization. The method is called right after the constructor and is typically used to instantiate variables or to set some properties to their starting values.

Listing 10-6 shows the LoadContent and UnloadContent methods. This is where all of the XNB files will get loaded into memory or unloaded from memory, depending on whether the game is starting or stopping, respectively. The LoadContent method is called after the Initialize method. UnloadContent is called when the game is quitting.

Listing 10-6. Load and Unload Methods

```
protected override void LoadContent()
{
    // Create a new SpriteBatch, which can be used to draw te
    _spriteBatch = new SpriteBatch(GraphicsDevice);

    // TODO: use this.Content to load your game content here
}

protected override void UnloadContent()
{
    // TODO: Unload any non ContentManager content here
}
```

Listing 10-7 shows the most interesting methods. Update and Draw are usually called 60 times per second (if your game is running at 60 frames per second). The Update method is where all game logic should go, such as collision detection, if bullets are hitting anything, if the player has any lives left, and so on. The Draw method is where the entire game gets drawn on the screen.

Listing 10-7. Update and Draw

```
protected override void Update(GameTime gameTime)
{
    // TODO: Add your update logic here

    base.Update(gameTime);
}

protected override void Draw(GameTime gameTime)
{
    GraphicsDevice.Clear(Color.CornflowerBlue);

    // TODO: Add your drawing code here

    base.Draw(gameTime);
}
```

Now that we have some idea of the structure of a game, let's start building one. The first thing we'll need is art, something to draw on the screen. We need a player, an enemy, and a bullet. I've drawn squares to function as the player and enemy here and a smaller square that looks like a shot from a laser pistol. Draw something up and save it as a PNG file. What we need to do now is create a new XNA project, either in Visual Studio 2010 or in Visual Studio 2012, with the Windows Phone 8 SDK installed. You'll notice that an XNA project consists of two projects: the game itself and a Content project. Add your art to that Content project, as shown in Figure 10-11.

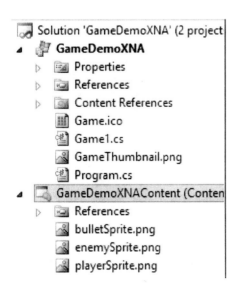

Figure 10-11. *The XNA project*

If we build this XNA project, our XNB files will be created; however, make sure that the project is set to Release mode instead of Debug or our game will fail certification when submitted to the Windows Store. Build the solution and go to the bin > Release folder of the project, as shown in Figure 10-12. It should contain the XNB files.

Figure 10-12. *The xnb files*

Add these files to the Content folder that we've added to our MonoGame solution a while back. Set the properties of the XNB files, as shown in Figure 10-13.

Figure 10-13. *Properties for XNB files*

This will ensure that when we build the project the XNB files are found in the correct location.

Adding the Model

It's time to add some classes to our game. I've added a folder to the project called Models where I'll put all my classes.

Player Class

We'll start with the Player class. We will use the code in Listing 10-8.

Listing 10-8. Player Class

```
public class Player : DrawableGameComponent
{
    public Texture2D Texture { get; set; }
    public Vector2 Position { get; set; }
    public bool IsAlive { get; set; }
    public int TimeTillNextShot { get; set; }

    private const int FireSpeed = 30;
```

```
    public Player(Game game)
        : base(game)
    {
        MouseManager.MouseMoved += MovePlayer;
        Position = new Vector2(0, 0);
        IsAlive = true;
    }

    protected override void LoadContent()
    {
        Texture = Game.Content.Load<Texture2D>(@"playerSprite");
        base.LoadContent();
    }

    private void MovePlayer(object sender, MouseMovedEventArgs mouseMovedEventArgs)
    {
        Position = new Vector2(mouseMovedEventArgs.Position.X, Position.Y);
    }

    public override void Update(GameTime gameTime)
    {
        TimeTillNextShot--;
    }

    public override void Draw(GameTime gameTime)
    {
        Game.SpriteBatch.Begin();
        Game.SpriteBatch.Draw(Texture, Position, Color.White);
        Game.SpriteBatch.End();

        base.Draw(gameTime);
    }

    public void ResetFireSpeed()
    {
        TimeTillNextShot = FireSpeed;
    }
}
```

As you can see in Listing 10-8, Player derives from DrawableGameComponent. MonoGame has two classes built for creating a model: GameComponent and DrawableGameComponent. The difference is that DrawableGameComponent has a Draw method and GameComponent does not. So when you're building a model for something that needs to be drawn on screen, it is best to use the DrawableGameComponent class. These classes have the same methods as the Game class. The difference is that the constructor, a class that derives from GameComponent or DrawableGameComponent, has a constructor with a parameter of type Game. That parameter is then passed into its base constructor. Once instantiated, the Update and Draw methods will be called 60 times per second in a 60-frames per second game, just like for the Game class.

On to the properties then. Texture2D is a class that will load in an XNB file. That class can then be used to draw the image on the screen. Vector2 is a vector that can be used to define a point on the screen. This is actually a bit special: a vector is not really a point in space, as shown in Figure 10-14, but its projection on the x axis and y axis can make it function like one.

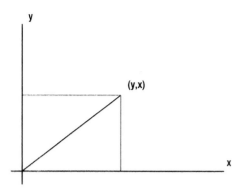

Figure 10-14. *A vector*

Vectors are used a lot in game development to determine the position of an object. In a 2D game, such as the one we're building here, we use a Vector2, which has an x and a y property. In a 3D game, we can use a Vector3, which also has an x and a y property, but it also has a z property to determine the depth of the vector.

After the Texture2D and the Vector2, we have a Boolean to check if the player is still alive. You'll see that this Boolean exists in the Player, Bullet, and Enemy classes. That's because both bullets and players will exist in a List<T> that we will iterate through in the Update method. Removing a bullet and an enemy from that list every time we shoot one would have a pretty big performance impact, so instead we just set the IsAlive Boolean to false. In the Draw method of enemy and bullet, we first check if it is alive before we draw it. TimeTillNextShot is used to prevent players from firing one big spree of bullets. The constant FireSpeed determines how long the player needs to wait between shots.

In the constructor, we add an event handler to the MouseMoved event (we'll have a look at the MouseManager in a minute). The position is set to 0,0, meaning the upper left corner of the screen. The correct position of the player will be set in the Game class itself. The last thing we do in the constructor is set the IsAlive Boolean to true.

In the LoadContent method, we load the XNB file into the Texture2D instance by using the ContentManager's Load method. The parameter we need to pass into that function is the file name of the XNB file without the extension.

The next method on the list is the event handler for the MouseMoved event. This will change the position of the player by setting the player's x coordinate equal to the mouse's x coordinate. Since in this type of game the player can only move horizontally, so we won't change its y coordinate.

The Update method for the player does nothing more than decrease the TimeTillNextShot property.

On to the Draw method then. Before we dive in here, there has been a small change to the Game class of the MonoGame framework. I've added a SpriteBatch property so that we can reuse that one throughout the game instead of initializing a new one every time we want to draw something, which can generate some serious memory issues. The property can be added either directly in the Game class if you're working with the MonoGame sources or through a partial class. Once that's done, you'll have access to Game.SpriteBatch. Before anything can be drawn, we need to call SpriteBatch.Begin, then call the SpriteBatch.Draw method, passing in the texture, position, and color. And to finish off we need to call SpriteBatch.End. And with that our first class is complete.

Enemy Class

Next we deal with the Enemy class, which is quite similar to the Player class. We will use the code in Listing 10-9.

Listing 10-9. Enemy Class

```
public class Enemy : DrawableGameComponent
    {
        public Rectangle CollRect { get; set; }
        public Texture2D Texture { get; set; }
```

```
        public Vector2 Position { get; set; }
        public bool IsAlive { get; set; }

        public Enemy(Game game)
            : base(game)
        {
        }

        public override void Initialize()
        {
            IsAlive = true;
            base.Initialize();
        }

        protected override void LoadContent()
        {
            Texture = Game.Content.Load<Texture2D>(@"enemySprite");
            CollRect = new Rectangle((int)Position.X, (int)Position.Y, Texture.Width, Texture.
Height);

            base.LoadContent();
        }

        public override void Draw(GameTime gameTime)
        {
            if (IsAlive)
            {
                Game.SpriteBatch.Begin();
                Game.SpriteBatch.Draw(Texture, Position, Color.White);
                Game.SpriteBatch.End();
            }

            base.Draw(gameTime);
        }
    }
```

The only new thing in this class compared with the Player class is the Rectangle CollRect. This is what we call a collision rectangle. The Rectangle class in MonoGame takes in an x and y coordinate where its upper left corner will be, followed by a width and a height. The rectangle itself will not be drawn, because it will not be visible on the screen. The useful part of this Rectangle class is the Intersects method, which will check if the rectangle intersects with another rectangle. What we'll do is place a rectangle around every enemy and every bullet. Then we will check if any bullet rectangle intersects with an enemy rectangle. If it does, that means the enemy has been hit and that both the enemy and the bullet should be destroyed. And here's one of the first things we tend to forget when playing games. It's not only the enemy that dies; the bullet should get destroyed as well or it will just keep going. But we'll dive into that when we're discussing the game logic. The rest of the Enemy class is similar to the Player class, except that this class doesn't use the MouseManager because our enemies don't respond to mouse movement.

Bullet Class

And on to the Bullet class we go. We will use the code provided in Listing 10-10.

Listing 10-10. Bullet Class

```
public class Bullet : DrawableGameComponent
    {
        public bool IsAlive { get; set; }
        public Vector2 Position { get; set; }
        public Texture2D Texture { get; set; }
        public Rectangle CollRect { get; set; }

        private const float Speed = 7f;

        public Bullet(Game game)
            : base(game)
        {
            Texture = Game.Content.Load<Texture2D>(@"bulletSprite");
            IsAlive = true;
        }

        public override void Update(GameTime gameTime)
        {
            if(!IsAlive) return;

            Position = new Vector2(Position.X, Position.Y - Speed);

            CollRect = new Rectangle((int)Position.X, (int)Position.Y, Texture.Width, Texture.Height);

            if (Position.Y < (0 - Texture.Height))
            {
                IsAlive = false;
            }
        }

        public override void Draw(GameTime gameTime)
        {
            if (IsAlive)
            {
                Game.SpriteBatch.Begin();
                Game.SpriteBatch.Draw(Texture, Position, Color.White);
                Game.SpriteBatch.End();
            }
            base.Draw(gameTime);
        }
    }
}
```

Once again a very similar class (we could've built a base class for all those properties that our three classes have in common, but this makes it easier for demo purposes). The Bullet class overrides the Update method from the DrawableGameComponent. As mentioned before, this method will get called 60 times per second if the game is running at 60 frames per second. What we do in the Update method is nothing when the bullet isn't alive, but when it is alive, we check its vertical position. If the bullet's y position is lower than zero, it means that the bullet has gone off screen and should no longer be updated or drawn. The framework won't do this for you, so we have to manually take these things into account. On some occasions we would want objects that are off screen to continue updating, for example, in a level where the player can freely run around with a camera scrolling over the level.

MouseManager class

With that, we've gone over the three objects that we'll use in this small game. In Listing 10-11, we'll have a look at the MouseManager, a helper class I use whenever I need mouse input in a MonoGame game.

Listing 10-11. MouseManager

```
public static class MouseManager
{
    private static Vector2 _mousePosition;
    private static Vector2 _previousPosition;

    public static event EventHandler<MouseMovedEventArgs> MouseMoved;
    public static event EventHandler MouseLeftButtonClicked;

    public static void UpdateMouse()
    {
        MouseState mouseState = Mouse.GetState();

        _mousePosition = new Vector2(mouseState.X, mouseState.Y);

        if (mouseState.LeftButton == ButtonState.Pressed)
        {
            if (MouseLeftButtonClicked == null) return;

            MouseLeftButtonClicked(null, new EventArgs());
        }

        // The mouse X and Y positions are returned relative to the top-left of the game window.
        if (_mousePosition != _previousPosition && _previousPosition != Vector2.Zero &&
MouseMoved != null)
        {
            if (_previousPosition.X < _mousePosition.X)
            {
                MouseMoved(null, new MouseMovedEventArgs(1, _mousePosition));
            }
            else
            {
                MouseMoved(null, new MouseMovedEventArgs(-1, _mousePosition));
            }
        }

        _previousPosition = _mousePosition;
    }
}
```

So how does this work? We get the MouseState from the mouse, which is a built-in class in MonoGame. We set the position to the _mousePosition vector. If the left mouse button is pressed, the MouseLeftButtonClicked event is fired if it has any attached event handlers. This UpdateMouse method will get called 60 times per second, just like the Update method, throughout the GameComponents, so we need to keep track of a previous position and determine if the current position is different. If it is different, we fire the MouseMoved event, passing in the new position and the direction it is moving into the MouseMovedEventArgs (as shown in Listing 10-12). To finish off, we set the current position to _previousPosition and we're done.

Listing 10-12. MouseMovedEventArgs

```
public class MouseMovedEventArgs : EventArgs
{
    //-1 for left, 1 for right
    public int Direction { get; set; }
    public Vector2 Position { get; set; }

    public MouseMovedEventArgs(int direction, Vector2 position)
    {
        Direction = direction;
        Position = position;
    }
}
```

The `MouseMovedEventArgs` has two properties: one for the mouse's current position and one for the direction, -1 being left and 1 being right. That's all the information we need to get this game playable.

Game Logic

It's time to have a look at the most interesting part of this game: the `Game` class, which holds all the logic. This file is called `Game1.cs` by default and, as mentioned earlier, it is the entry point of the game. Listing 10-13 shows some fields, the player, a list of bullets, and a list of enemies.

Listing 10-13. Fields in Game1.cs

```
GraphicsDeviceManager _graphics;
private Player _player;
private List<Bullet> _bullets;
private List<Enemy> _enemies;
```

Easy enough, so on to more interesting stuff in Listing 10-14.

Listing 10-14. Initialize Method

```
protected override void Initialize()
{
    MouseManager.MouseLeftButtonClicked += Fire;
    _player = new Player(this);
    Components.Add(_player);

    //position the player
    _player.Position = new Vector2((GraphicsDevice.Viewport.Width / 2) - (_player.Texture.Width / 2),
GraphicsDevice.Viewport.Height - _player.Texture.Height);

    _bullets = new List<Bullet>();
    _enemies = new List<Enemy>();

    LoadEnemies();

    base.Initialize();
}
```

191

In this method, we attach an event handler for a left-mouse button click. We initialize the Player class and add it to the Components collection. All items in this collection need to be derived from either the GameComponent the or DrawableGameComponent. Putting them in this collection will ensure that their Draw and Update methods are called over and over as long as the game is running. We set the player at the bottom middle of the screen. We initialize the collections that will hold the bullets and enemies and call the LoadEnemies method, which is shown in Listing 10-15.

Listing 10-15. LoadEnemies Method

```
private void LoadEnemies()
{
    _enemies.Add(new Enemy(this) { Position = new Vector2(20, 20) });
    _enemies.Add(new Enemy(this) { Position = new Vector2(149, 20) });
    _enemies.Add(new Enemy(this) { Position = new Vector2(298, 20) });

    foreach (var enemy in _enemies)
    {
        Components.Add(enemy);
    }
}
```

In a real game, this would be a bit more complicated, but here we are just adding three enemies on a fixed position and adding them to the Components collection of the game. Listing 10-16 shows the code for the Update method.

Listing 10-16. Update Method

```
protected override void Update(GameTime gameTime)
{
    MouseManager.UpdateMouse();

    foreach (var bullet in _bullets.Where(bullet => bullet.IsAlive))
    {
        foreach (var enemy in _enemies)
        {
            if (enemy.CollRect.Intersects(bullet.CollRect))
            {
                enemy.IsAlive = false;
                bullet.IsAlive = false;

                break;
            }
        }
    }

    base.Update(gameTime);
}
```

The first thing we do in the Update method is call the UpdateMouse method on the MouseManager. MouseManager is not a GameComponent, so calling the Update method is not handled by the framework. After updating the mouse, we start iterating through all the bullets. For every bullet, we iterate through the list of enemies checking if an enemy's collision rectangle intersects with a bullet's rectangle. If it does, we kill the bullet and the enemy and break the loop. That's all there is to this game's logic. In a real game, this method tends to get pretty big, so make sure to document every part really well with comments because it's easy to get lost in it over time. Listing 10-17 shows what happens when the player clicks the left mouse button to fire a bullet.

Listing 10-17. Firing a Bullet

```
private void Fire(object sender, EventArgs eventArgs)
{
    if (_player.TimeTillNextShot <= 0)
    {
        Bullet newBullet = new Bullet(this)
                            {
                                Position = _player.Position,
                                IsAlive = true
                            };

        Components.Add(newBullet);
        _bullets.Add(newBullet);

        _player.ResetFireSpeed();
    }
}
```

The first thing we need to do when trying to fire a bullet is check if the player is allowed to fire, whether enough time has passed since the last shot. If that checks out, we declare a new bullet, starting from the player's current position, set it to alive, and add it to the Components collection. Don't forget to add it to our own _bullets collection and call the ResetFireSpeed method on the player object.

The Draw method in our main Game class is empty since every object is taking care of its drawing itself.

And with that our very simplistic game is ready. Go ahead and play it! Then get out there and build a nice looking, addictive game!

Summary

This chapter discussed the out-of-the-box methods for building games for the Windows Store. This requires either C++ or JavaScript skills, which is something not every C# developer knows. We've taken a look at community-driven projects, in particular MonoGame. MonoGame is an open source implementation of the XNA classes and namespaces, allowing C# developers to build great looking games in a language with which they are very familiar.

Building games can be fun and challenging. History has proven over and over that you don't need extreme 3D modeling skills to build a successful game, just look at Angry Birds! The concept is really old, the graphics look very kiddy, and the creators are making millions off it.

The best advice I can give you is to build a game that you would like to play yourself. And build it so that it feels just right for you, then get it out there. Games generally sell quite well, even the really small ones (except for the one we've built here obviously). So get to it!

The next chapter will explain how to upload a project to the Windows Store.

CHAPTER 11

The Windows Store

Congratulations! You've made it to the most exciting part of the journey of app building: submitting the app to the app store. In this case, that means the Windows Store. Whether you're a first-time app developer or a seasoned one with tons of apps across multiple platforms and ecosystems, this remains an exciting moment. After days, weeks, or even months of building, fine tuning, and perfecting a piece of software that sprouted from your imagination, it's time to send your code in for certification.

Before your app becomes available on the Windows Store, however, it needs to pass a series of both automated and manual tests. For this purpose, Microsoft has an entire test team available that does nothing else but thoroughly testing apps all day, every day. Apps first go through some automated tests that we can run for ourselves upfront (more about that later). Second, the app gets deployed onto a wide range of devices, from desktops to laptops, tablets, and hybrids all running Windows 8 or Windows RT. Once the app is deployed, it gets tested; every button is pressed, every possible way of navigating is done, and every service call gets called. These people get paid to make your app crash, so it is up to the developers to ensure they fail their mission.

After a few days with the testing team, your app will either pass or fail certification. If it fails, you'll receive a nice report stating why it failed and what you can do about it. We'll go over the most common reasons for failure later in this chapter. Once your app passes certification, it will be available in the store either immediately or on the date you've designated when submitting your app.

This chapter will walk you through creating a developer account, preparing your app for submitting, and actually submitting the app, as well as explain the different business models that are available on the Windows Store.

Creating a Developer Account

To start selling applications on the Windows Store, you need to establish a developer account. You do this via the Windows 8 portal, and the registration link is conveniently linked inside Visual Studio 2012. In Visual Studio 2012 Express, there's a Store menu item, while in the paid versions of Visual Studio 2012 it's found under PROJECT ➤ Store, as shown in Figure 11-1. Launching this will take you to the developer registration screen, as shown in Figure 11-2.

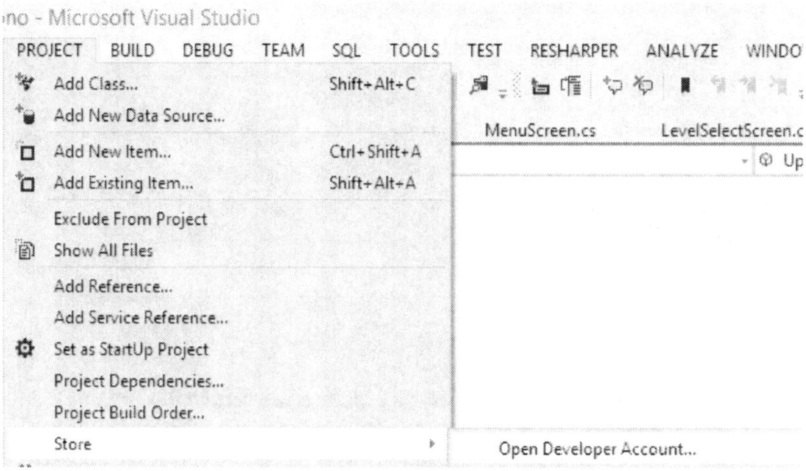

Figure 11-1. The store menu

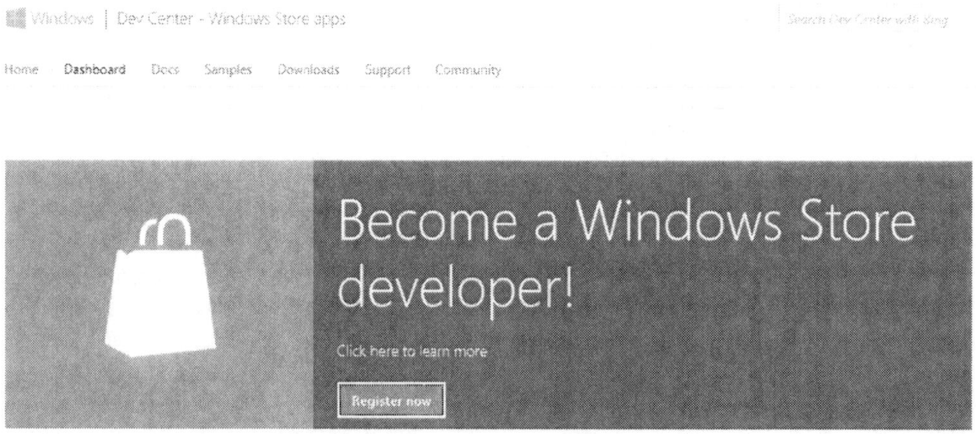

Figure 11-2. The Windows Store web site

The first step in the registration process is to provide your personal information, postal address, phone number, and so forth. It is important that you fill this in correctly as your identity will be verified before you can receive any payment from apps in the Windows Store. You'll also need to fill out some tax forms before you can receive payouts. Also note that not every country allows the selling of apps. The information on this can be found at http://msdn.microsoft.com/en-US/library/windows/apps/jj193593. On the store web site, at the bottom of the web page, you'll need to select your developer name. That's the name that will be visible on the store as the developer of the app, so choose wisely my young Padawan! The site will tell you whether your preferred developer name is still available.

The next page is the license agreement. As always, you're supposed to read it fully and agree with what's stated there. The third step allows you to enter promotional codes that you might have received somewhere. If you don't have a code, you will need to pay an annual registration fee and you will be prompted to select a payment method. At this time, only credit card payment is available. Enter the required details, click next, confirm the purchase, and you're golden!

Congratulations! You are now a registered Windows 8 developer. The Windows 8 developer portal allows you to register your app name even before you submit it. Once you register an app name it stays reserved for one year. If you haven't submitted the app by the end of that year then the name gets released. So if you have an idea for an app, register the name before anyone else does. Keep in mind that Windows 8 will be used by millions, and some are probably developers just like you. So it's really important to register that name. Reserving an app name is again done from the store menu in Visual Studio 2012, as shown in Figure 11-3.

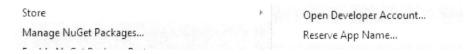

Figure 11-3. *Reserve an app name*

That menu item will take you to the developer portal and into the app submission wizard, as shown in Figure 11-4. To reserve an app name, you only need to complete the first part of the wizard, and the other steps can be completed once your app is ready to submit.

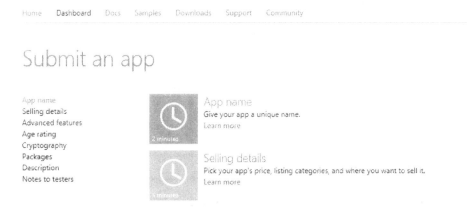

Figure 11-4. *The submit an app wizard*

After entering your app name and clicking Save, you'll notice that the app has appeared on the dashboard and is marked as "Incomplete," as shown in Figure 11-5. That means you haven't gone through the entire submit wizard yet, but it also means that the app name is reserved for you, so good job there!

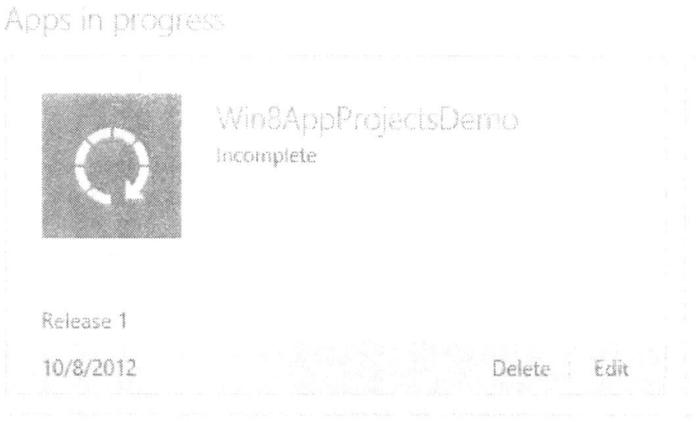

Apps in progress

Win8AppProjectsDemo
Incomplete

Release 1

10/8/2012   Delete   Edit

Figure 11-5. *An app as it appears on your dashboard*

Prepare to Submit Your App

As your app reaches completion, you might feel compelled to rush it along to what you feel is complete and submit it to the store. It's really important that you stay calm and really test your app so you won't get a certification failure, which would amount to three to seven days where no one can download or buy your app only because you rushed it. This section of the chapter will go over some of the most common reasons for certification failure.

The biggest reason to fail certification, and I do speak from experience here (multiple times actually), is the privacy policy. The moment the Internet (client) capability is checked in your app manifest, you need to specify a privacy policy stating that your app contacts the Internet, why it does that, and what information is saved by the service that is contacted. You can either integrate the policy into your app or provide a link to a web page containing the policy from the app. What's important is that the policy can be found from within the app, and this is usually done from the Settings charm (see Chapter 5 on how to implement the Settings charm). To get you started, here's the basic privacy policy I use for my apps. Feel free to use this text as a starting point for your own policy.

EXAMPLE PRIVACY POLICY

We only collect information that we get from your use of our services. This information includes only logging information: when you use our services, we may automatically collect and store certain information in server logs. This information can include the date of your search query, the search query itself, and the IP address of the device used to connect to the service.

We need to log information to check what went wrong in case of an error, or how many requests are being processed at a given time to detect load issues.

We will not share this information with any other organization or person, except if we're required to do so based on legal inquiries.

This Privacy Policy can change at any time, the continued use of the application constitutes acceptance of any such change.

Another common reason to fail submission is when your app contacts an external service and it can't handle when the device doesn't have an active network or Internet connection. This is one of the first things that the test team checks. Checking for an Internet connection is really easy. Listing 11-1 provides the code to check for a network connection.

Listing 11-1. Checking Network Connection

```
if (!NetworkInterface.GetIsNetworkAvailable())
{
    MessageDialog dialog = new MessageDialog("No active internetconnection found, please connect
to the internet and try again");
    dialog.ShowAsync();

    throw new WebException("No connection");
}
```

This code provides your user with a nice error message and throws an exception that you can easily catch.

Also make sure that you have an app that actually does something. This may sound silly, but the test team actually receives "Hello, world" style apps on a regular basis. Those apps obviously aren't allowed on the Windows Store.

Another area of common failure, if your app requires a user to sign in, is that you must provide a sign-in button. Also you must provide a test account for the test team. They won't even test your app if you don't provide one, and they won't go through the hassle of creating an account and possibly risk providing personal information from their testers.

Also in the list of usual suspects for failure, your app cannot crash at any time under any circumstance when being tested. If your app might throw an exception when the user faces east standing on one leg while the device faces south on a rainy day, provide an exception handler. Also, your app must work great both with touch controls and with mouse and keyboard. You must use the simulator to test this or use an actual touch device.

For a complete overview of all the certification rules, take a look at the "Resolving certification errors (Windows)" page on the Microsoft web site: `http://msdn.microsoft.com/en-us/library/windows/apps/hh921583.aspx`.

When you think your app is ready, you can run the Windows App Certification Kit (WACK). WACK is a series of automated tests and is the first thing that the test team does when it starts testing your app. To start the WACK tests from within Visual Studio (with your solution opened), go to PROJECT ➤ Store ➤ Create App Packages, as shown in Figure 11-6. Or you can just find it on the Windows 8 start screen.

Open Developer Account...

Reserve App Name...

Acquire Developer License...

Edit App Manifest

Associate App with the Store...

Capture Screenshots...

Create App Packages...

Figure 11-6. *Create App Packages menu*

Visual Studio will ask you if you want to build a package that you're going to submit to the store, as shown in Figure 11-7. If you want to run the WACK, you need to select Yes and sign in with your Live ID.

Figure 11-7. *Create package wizard*

Once you sign in, follow the wizard all the way through. At the end you'll get the option to launch the WACK, as shown in Figure 11-8.

Figure 11-8. *WACK hard at work*

The process takes a few minutes, and your app will launch a few times. When it does, do not interact with it. Just leave your device running while the tests do their thing. When it finishes, you get a Passed or Failed message, as shown in Figure 11-9.

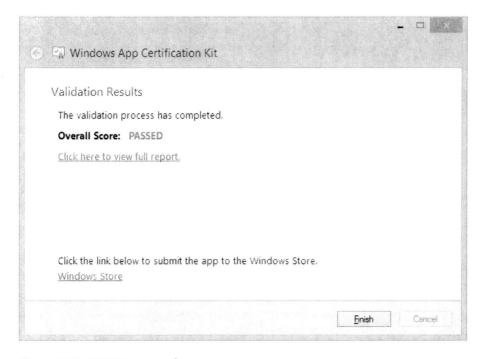

Figure 11-9. *WACK tests passed*

If it fails, you can look at the report and see why it failed. Make sure this test passes before you submit your app to the marketplace.

Submit Your App

After successfully passing the WACK, it's time to submit your app to the marketplace. Submitting an app is quite easy. To get started, select Upload App Packages from the by now familiar store menu in Visual Studio 2012, as shown in Figure 11-10.

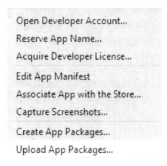

Figure 11-10. *Upload Package menu item*

This will open the Windows 8 development portal on the same page where you reserved an app name earlier. Only this time we're going to complete all the steps instead of only the first, as shown in Figure 11-11.

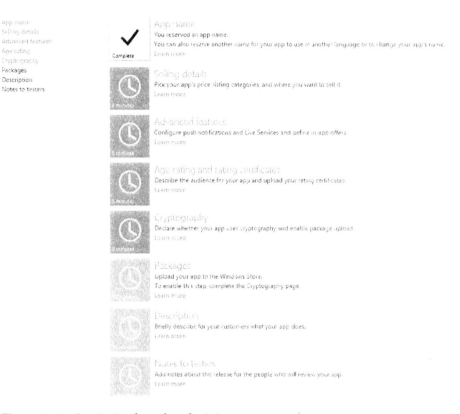

Figure 11-11. *Continuing down the submission process*

The first step, after selecting an app name, is to specify the selling details. On this page you can select the countries where you want your app to be available. Be careful with the countries you select, because some countries have rules on what's allowed inside an app. We also need to select when the app should be published onto the store: immediately after certification passes or on a set date. We also set the category where our app will appear and the hardware requirements to use the app. The hardware requirements are mostly for graphic-intensive apps, such as games that require a certain set of DirectX capabilities that are not supported by all graphic cards.

The next step is to define the advanced features. In this step, push notifications and in app purchases are configured. For each item we want to sell in our apps, we need to add an item here. This area is depressingly short and easy for something named "advanced." Don't worry, the wizard guides you all the way.

Next up is setting the age rating. There are multiple options here, each very well documented, so I'm going to go the lazy route here and just copy it from the portal, as shown in Figure 11-12.

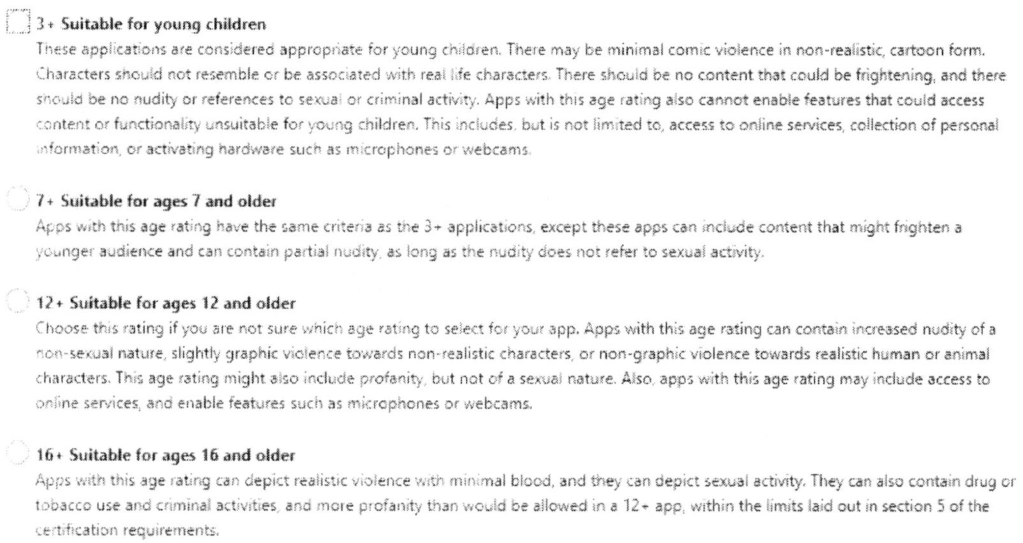

☐ **3+ Suitable for young children**

These applications are considered appropriate for young children. There may be minimal comic violence in non-realistic, cartoon form. Characters should not resemble or be associated with real life characters. There should be no content that could be frightening, and there should be no nudity or references to sexual or criminal activity. Apps with this age rating also cannot enable features that could access content or functionality unsuitable for young children. This includes, but is not limited to, access to online services, collection of personal information, or activating hardware such as microphones or webcams.

○ **7+ Suitable for ages 7 and older**

Apps with this age rating have the same criteria as the 3+ applications, except these apps can include content that might frighten a younger audience and can contain partial nudity, as long as the nudity does not refer to sexual activity.

○ **12+ Suitable for ages 12 and older**

Choose this rating if you are not sure which age rating to select for your app. Apps with this age rating can contain increased nudity of a non-sexual nature, slightly graphic violence towards non-realistic characters, or non-graphic violence towards realistic human or animal characters. This age rating might also include profanity, but not of a sexual nature. Also, apps with this age rating may include access to online services, and enable features such as microphones or webcams.

○ **16+ Suitable for ages 16 and older**

Apps with this age rating can depict realistic violence with minimal blood, and they can depict sexual activity. They can also contain drug or tobacco use and criminal activities, and more profanity than would be allowed in a 12+ app, within the limits laid out in section 5 of the certification requirements.

Figure 11-12. *Age ratings*

Choose wisely. The lower the age, the greater the limitations are. For some regions, you might require an age certificate if you're publishing a game. You can find information about creating an age certificate on Microsoft's web page "Obtaining a game rating certificate (Windows)":
http://msdn.microsoft.com/en-us/library/windows/apps/hh452763.aspx.

The cryptography step is just a simple Yes/No question, unless you answer yes. If you use any form of encryption, you need to specify it here. This is required by U.S. law, not something that Microsoft invented. If you select Yes, the wizard asks you if it's used only for user authentication, copy protection, Digital Rights Management (DRM), or signatures. If you use cryptography for anything else, you will need to request an export commodity classification number and enter it on this page.

Now we're getting into the exciting parts! It's time to upload the app package. If you created a package before, you should find a subfolder named AppPackages in your Solution folder. In that subfolder, you'll find your created package, waiting to be uploaded. Either drag and drop it onto the web page or browse it using the Select file dialog from the site.

Almost there! Time to describe your app. The information you enter here is the information that will appear on the Windows Store. We need to enter a description, some bullet points about the features of the app, and some keywords (these are used when users search for an app with a keyword). We also need to provide at least one screenshot and an e-mail address that our users can use to get support. If you have a privacy policy, do not forget to provide a link to it here.

As a final step, we can add some notes to testers. This is the place to specify test credentials should your app require them. And with that completely filled out, it's time to hit submit, wait a couple of days for the testing to complete, and be very proud when you see your first app on the Windows Store.

Summary

This chapter examined all the required steps to get your app into the Windows Store. The biggest pitfall in this process is the WACK, which is something you can, and should, run yourself before you submit your application. It verifies things like your application icons, if the app launches with or without a working network connection. Another common reason for failure is the lack of a privacy policy. As soon as your app contacts the Internet, even if just for analytics or advertisements, you will need a privacy policy page. This can be within the app, but you will also need a web page because the privacy policy needs to be reachable both from within the app and from the store.

We discussed the importance of selecting an age rating and the countries where your app will be available. Not every app will be allowed in all countries, some have very strict rules about app content. When you're sure that everything's in order, go ahead and submit your app!

The time between submitting the app and the app being in the store is currently about three to four days. If your app fails submission, you add another three to four days. So test very thoroughly before submitting. A time will come when one of your apps fails submission. Don't feel bad about it! Read the report, fix the errors, resubmit, and most importantly, learn from this failed submission.

Index

■ N, O, P, Q

■ R

■ S

CPSIA information can be obtained at www.ICGtesting.com
Printed in the USA
LVOW111219020313

322389LV00025B/300/P